Influence

Life Together Resources

Building Character Together series

Authenticity: Living a Spiritually Healthy Life

Friendship: Living a Connected Life

Faith: Living a Transformed Life

Service: Living a Meaningful Life

Influence: Living a Contagious Life

Obedience: Living a Yielded Life

Doing Life Together series

Beginning Life Together

Connecting with God's Family

Growing to Be Like Christ

Developing Your SHAPE to Serve Others

Sharing Your Life Mission Every Day

Surrendering Your Life to God's Pleasure

Experiencing Christ Together series

Beginning in Christ Together

Connecting in Christ Together

Growing in Christ Together

Serving Like Christ Together

Sharing Christ Together

Surrendering to Christ Together

building
CHARACTER
together

INFLUENCE

living a

Contagious

life

BRETT and DEE EASTMAN
TODD and DENISE WENDORFF

ZONDERVAN®

ZONDERVAN.com/
AUTHORTRACKER
follow your favorite authors

Influence
Copyright © 2007 by Brett and Deanna Eastman, Todd and Denise Wendorff

Requests for information should be addressed to:

Zondervan, *Grand Rapids, Michigan 49530*

ISBN-10: 0-310-24994-5
ISBN-13: 978-0-310-24994-8

Interior design by Melissa Elenbaas

Printed in the United States of America

07 08 09 10 11 12 13 • 10 9 8 7 6 5 4 3 2 1

Contents

ACKNOWLEDGMENTS

It's been quite a ride ever since our first series was published back in 2002. Literally thousands of churches and small groups have studied the LIFE TOGETHER series to the tune of over two million copies sold. As we said back in our first series, "By the grace of God and a clear call on the hearts of a few, our dream has become a reality." Now, our dream has entered the realm of being beyond all that we could ask or imagine.

To see thousands and thousands of people step out to gather a few friends and do a Bible study with an easy-to-use DVD curriculum has been amazing. People have grown in their faith, introduced their friends to Christ, and found deeper connection with God. Thanks to God for planting this idea in our hearts. Thanks to all of those who took a risk by stepping out to lead a group for six weeks for the very first time. This has been truly amazing.

Once again, a great team was instrumental to creating this new series in community. From the start back at Saddleback with Todd and Denise Wendorff and Brett and Dee Eastman, the writing team has grown. Special thanks to John Fischer, yes, THE John Fischer, for writing all of the introductions to these studies. Also, thanks to our LIFE TOGETHER writing team: Pam Marotta, Peggy Matthews Rose, and Teri Haymaker. Last, but not least, thanks to Allen White for keeping this project on track and getting the ball in the net.

Thank you to our church families who have loved and supported us and helped us grow over the years. There are so many pastors, staff, and members that have taught us so much. We love you all.

Finally, thank you to our beloved families who have lived with us, laughed at us, and loved us through it all. We love doing our lives together with you.

OUTLINE OF
EACH SESSION

Most people want to live a healthy, balanced spiritual life, but few achieve this by themselves. And most small groups struggle to balance all of God's purposes in their meetings. Groups tend to overemphasize one of the five purposes, perhaps fellowship or discipleship. Rarely is there a healthy balance that includes evangelism, ministry, and worship. That's why we've included all of these elements in this study so you can live a healthy, balanced spiritual life over time.

A typical group session will include the following:

 CONNECTING WITH GOD'S FAMILY (FELLOWSHIP). The foundation for spiritual growth is an intimate connection with God and his family. A few people who really know you and who earn your trust provide a place to experience the life Jesus invites you to live. This section of each session typically offers you two options: You can get to know your whole group by using the icebreaker question, or you can check in with one or two group members — your spiritual partner(s) — for a deeper connection and encouragement in your spiritual journey.

 GROWING TO BE LIKE CHRIST (DISCIPLESHIP). Here is where you come face-to-face with Scripture. In core passages you'll explore what the Bible teaches about character through the lives of God's people in Scripture. The focus won't be on accumulating information but on how we should live in light of the Word of God. We want to help you apply the Scriptures practically, creatively, and from your heart as well as your head. At the end of the day, allowing the timeless truths from God's Word to transform our lives in Christ is our greatest aim.

FOR DEEPER STUDY. If you want to dig deeper into more Bible passages about the topic at hand, we've provided additional passages and questions. Your group may choose to do study homework ahead of each meeting in order to cover more biblical material. Or you as an individual may choose to study the For Deeper Study passages on your own. If you prefer not to do study homework, the Growing section will

provide you with plenty to discuss within the group. These options allow individuals or the whole group to go deeper in their study, while still accommodating those who can't do homework.

You can record your discoveries in your journal. We encourage you to read some of your insights to a friend (spiritual partner) for accountability and support. Spiritual partners may check in each week over the phone, through email, or at the beginning of the group meeting.

 DEVELOPING YOUR GIFTS TO SERVE OTHERS (MINISTRY). Jesus trained his disciples to discover and develop their gifts to serve others. God has designed you uniquely to serve him in a way no other person can. This section will help you discover and use your God-given design. It will also encourage your group to discover your unique design as a community. In this study, you'll put into practice what you've learned in the Bible study by taking a step to serve others. These simple steps will take your group on a faith journey that could change your lives forever.

 SHARING YOUR LIFE MISSION EVERY DAY (EVANGELISM). Many people skip over this aspect of the Christian life because it's scary, relationally awkward, or simply too much work for their busy schedules. But Jesus wanted all of his disciples to help outsiders connect with him, to know him personally. This doesn't mean preaching on street corners. It could mean welcoming a few newcomers into your group, hosting a short-term group in your home, or walking through this study with a friend. In this study, you'll have an opportunity to go beyond Bible study to biblical living.

 SURRENDERING YOUR LIFE FOR GOD'S PLEASURE (WORSHIP). God is most pleased by a heart that is fully his. Each group session will give you a chance to surrender your heart to God in prayer and worship. You may read a psalm together, share a page in your journal, or sing a song to close your meeting. (A LIFE TOGETHER Worship DVD/CD series, produced by Maranatha!, is available through www.lifetogether. com.) If you have never prayed aloud in a group before, no one will put pressure on you. Instead, you'll experience the support of others who are praying for you. This time will knit your hearts in community and help you surrender your hurts and dreams into the hands of the One who knows you best.

STUDY NOTES. This section provides background notes on the Bible passage(s) you examine in the Growing section. You may want to refer to these notes during your group meeting or as a reference for those doing additional study.

REFLECTIONS. Each week on the Reflections pages we provide Scriptures to read and reflect on between group meetings. We suggest you use this section to seek God at home throughout the week. This time at home should begin and end with prayer. Don't get in a hurry; take enough time to hear God's direction.

SUBGROUPS FOR DISCUSSION AND PRAYER. In some of the sessions of this series we have suggested you separate into groups of two to four for discussion or prayer. This is to assure greater participation and deeper discussion.

FESTIVE INFLUENCE—
LEVI, JESUS, AND THE SINNERS

We moved to New England a number of years ago when our family was just beginning, and my wife and I went with a commitment to invest in our neighborhood community. Our goal was to be in relationships with people in general without distinction as to their beliefs. This was new for me, having grown up fairly isolated in a protective evangelical environment.

Through my wife's involvement in the leadership of the local YWCA and the Chamber of Commerce, we soon developed a relationship with four other couples that grew into a monthly get-together we called the Dancing Fools night. It all started when the ten of us had dinner at one of our homes and ended up putting music on and dancing our socks off. We had so much fun, we decided to meet again at someone else's house and thus began a little round robin tradition. Though these evenings were formed around fun, they also deepened our relationships and strengthened our faith message whenever we shared it.

We no longer live in this community, but we think of the Dancing Fools often and remember this experience as a model of the kind of relationships that are possible if we just extend ourselves a little beyond our comfort zones. I think I was the one who learned the most, having been almost brainwashed by my upbringing to dislike non-Christians. I found out what beautiful people God has created, and how opportunities to be a fragrance of Christ are a natural result of simply and genuinely loving people for who they are.

CONNECTING WITH GOD'S FAMILY   20 MIN.

Given the choice, most of us would rather party with our Christian friends than hang out with those unfamiliar with or even hostile to our spiritual beliefs. But who would Jesus have us spending our time on earth with? In this lesson, we'll look at how Jesus set the example for us when it comes to outreach.

1. Take some time now to briefly share with the group how you came to be here today. Tell how you usually respond when invited to parties or other social events with people you don't know.

2. Open to the Small Group Agreement on pages 89–90 of the appendix. Take a few minutes to review the group values listed there before you begin this study. These values will help everyone know what to expect and how to contribute to a meaningful small group. It's a good idea to choose one or two values your group can focus on to guide you through this study and help you build deeper friendships. If you are new to the group or the group is new, you may find helpful the Frequently Asked Questions section on pages 86–88.

3. While you are working through the rest of this session, begin collecting information from everyone for your Small Group Roster that is found on pages 120–121. Pass it around the circle and have everyone write down their contact information. Ask someone to make copies or type up a list with everyone's information and email it to the group this week.

GROWING TO BE LIKE CHRIST   40 MIN.

Jesus was our model for evangelism. Knowing his time on earth would be brief, he packed every moment with significance. Jesus understood his purpose; he knew why the Father had sent him.

In Luke 5:27–32 we find Jesus on his way from having healed a paralyzed man brought to him by friends who'd heard Jesus was preaching nearby. By this time, Jesus' reputation was clearly growing and the local religious leaders (the Pharisees) were not happy about it. Who was this man, breaking all their rules and stirring people up so? Some were even saying he was the long-promised Messiah!

Because of our need to feel accepted and control the outcomes in our lives, we would understand if Jesus had gone to the religious leaders to explain himself or try to win them over somehow. Instead, he caught the attention of one of the most hated men in the community—a tax collector. Tax collectors were often seen as people who betrayed their fellow Jews by taking money from them to give to the Roman government. What an unlikely candidate for salvation! Or was he?

"Levi," Jesus said, "follow me." And Levi, better known to us as the apostle Matthew, did exactly as Jesus said. It couldn't have been a casual decision, for the Bible tells us Matthew left everything behind to follow Jesus.

In his joy over his new life, Matthew threw a party for Jesus. Rather than inviting the local religious and community leaders, Scripture tells us he invited his fellow tax collectors and others the Pharisees described as "sinners."

"Why?" the Pharisees demanded to know. "How can you consort with these people?" The Pharisees saw themselves as paragons of religious virtue. But Jesus knew both those who needed to hear his truth ... and those who would listen.

Read Luke 5:27–32:

> After this, Jesus went out and saw a tax collector by the name of Levi sitting at his tax booth. "Follow me," Jesus said to him, [28] and Levi got up, left everything and followed him. [29] Then Levi held a great banquet for Jesus at his house, and a large crowd of tax collectors and others were eating with them. [30] But the Pharisees and the teachers of the law who belonged to their sect complained to his disciples, "Why do you eat and drink with tax collectors and 'sinners'?" [31] Jesus answered them, "It is not the healthy who need a doctor, but the sick. [32] I have not come to call the righteous, but sinners to repentance."

4. Discuss the ways in which Matthew, in this passage, is an example to all believers.

5. What do you make of the fact that Matthew left everything to follow Jesus (Luke 5:28)? Does God always ask us to leave our old lives behind?

6. Verse 29 tells us that Levi (Matthew) "held a great banquet" for Jesus. What clue does this provide as to Matthew's life and what he was leaving behind?

7. In our world of celebrities and people with answers for every ailment, it's easy for us to be enticed to follow especially charismatic leaders. How do you think we can know which ones are genuine and which are false?

8. In his joy at meeting Jesus, Matthew invited all his tax collector friends to come and meet him too. Once we have discovered Jesus and begun to follow him, what responsibility do you think we have toward others who do not know him?

9. What type of attitude do you think it takes to refer to another person as a "sinner"?

   How difficult is it to cultivate this attitude?

10. Matthew understood what Jesus wanted all of us to see in ourselves—that we are all sinners in need of a Savior. Where do you think we discover this mind-set?

11. Jesus said to the Pharisees, "It is not the healthy who need a doctor, but the sick. I have not come to call the righteous, but sinners to repentance." To repent means "to turn around," or "to change one's mind." What does repentance look like in a person's life? What must we recognize about ourselves for repentance to occur?

12. How do you think seeing ourselves as sinners in need of repentance influences our character development?

FOR DEEPER STUDY

Matthew did not turn from his friends when he turned toward Jesus; he invited them to join him. Look at Matthew 4:19. What did Jesus say about his expectations for our lives and relationships?

How can this be reconciled with 2 Corinthians 6:14, which warns us not to be unequally yoked, or partnered, with unbelievers? See 1 Corinthians 5:9–13 for help.

DEVELOPING YOUR GIFTS TO SERVE OTHERS   10 MIN.

13. Pair up with someone in your group. (We suggest that men partner with men and women with women.) This person will be your "spiritual partner" during this study. This person will support and encourage you to complete any goals you set for yourself in the coming weeks. Following through on a resolution is tough when you're on your own, but we've found it makes all the difference to have a partner cheering us on.

On pages 92–93 is a Personal Health Plan, a chart for keeping track of your spiritual progress. In the box that says

"WHO are you connecting with spiritually?" write your partner's name. You can see that the Health Plan contains space for you to record the ups and downs of your progress each week in the column labeled "My Progress." And now with your spiritual partner, you don't have to do it alone but together with a friend.

For now, don't worry about the WHAT, WHERE, WHEN, and HOW questions on your Health Plan.

14. Everywhere Jesus went he used stories, or parables, to demonstrate our need for salvation. Through these stories, he helped people see the error of their ways, leading them to turn to him. Your story can be just as powerful today. Turn to Telling Your Story on pages 98–99 of the appendix. Review this with your spiritual partner. Begin to develop your story by sharing what your life was like before you knew Christ. (If you haven't yet committed your life to Christ or are not sure, you can find information about this in the Surrendering section. If you became a Christian at a very young age and don't remember what life was like before Christ, reflect on what you have seen in the life of someone close to you.) Make notes about this aspect of your story below and commit to writing it out this week.

SHARING YOUR LIFE MISSION EVERY DAY   10 MIN.

Luke 5:28 tells us Matthew left everything to follow Jesus. In Matthew's brief story here, we see that his encounter with Christ completely changed his life.

15. Briefly share your life-changing encounter with the Lord. Pray for opportunities this week to share your story with at least one other person who needs to meet Jesus.

16. Use the Circles of Life diagram to help you think of neighbors, family members, friends, or coworkers who don't yet know Christ. Write at least two names in each circle. We will take time to pray for these people in the Surrendering section.

CIRCLES OF LIFE

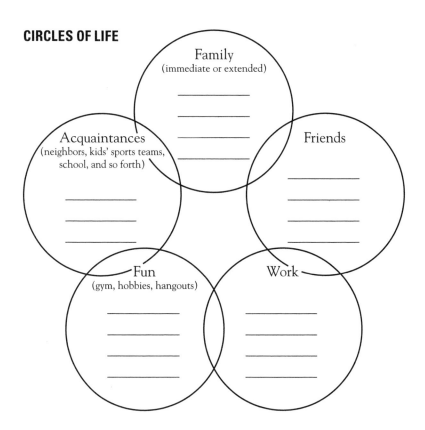

17. If you have never invited Jesus to take control of your life, why not ask him in now? If you are not clear about God's gift of eternal life for everyone who believes in Jesus and how to receive this gift, take a minute to pray and ask God to help you understand what he wants you to do about trusting in Jesus. Then read the following verses, taking time to pray for understanding of each one of them.

For all have sinned and fall short of the glory of God. (Romans 3:23)

But God demonstrates his own love for us in this: While we were still sinners, Christ died for us. (Romans 5:8)

For the wages of sin is death, but the gift of God is eternal life in Christ Jesus our Lord. (Romans 6:23)

If you confess with your mouth, "Jesus is Lord," and believe in your heart that God raised him from the dead, you will be saved. For it is with your heart that you believe and are justified, and it is with your mouth that you confess and are saved. (Romans 10:9–10)

Everyone who calls on the name of the Lord will be saved. (Romans 10:13)

If you believe that Jesus died in your place to pay the penalty for your sins and to provide for you eternal life in God's presence, you can receive him into your life right now. Pray the following prayer, or one like it, agreeing with God that you have sinned and you need his forgiveness. Ask Jesus to come into your life, to make you the person he wants you to be, and provide you with eternal life with him.

"Dear God, I know I haven't been living for you, but for myself. I believe Jesus died on the cross to pay for my sins. I need you in my life and I want to live the rest of my life the way you want me to. Please put your Spirit into my life to guide me. I want to receive the forgiveness you made available to me through Jesus' sacrifice. Come into

my life now, Lord. I want to follow you all the days of my life. Amen."

If you sincerely prayed asking Jesus to come into your life, you can trust him with the rest of your life and beyond. Share your decision with someone, maybe your small group leader or someone in the group. Give someone the chance to rejoice with you and encourage you in your spiritual growth.

18. Share your prayer requests with the group. Then close your time together by praying for one another. Ask God to give you opportunities this week to share what your life was like before Christ with the people on your list. Remember, God's power is available to meet your needs. Write down group members' prayer requests on the Prayer and Praise Report page on page 22.

19. Note the Reflections pages at the end of this session. Use these in your quiet time this week. There are five daily Scripture readings from the study and a place to record your summary of the five reflections on day six. Record any thoughts or direction you receive from the Lord in the space provided.

STUDY NOTES

A tax collector. The tax system under the Romans was wrought with corruption. The position of tax collector was auctioned to the highest bidder, who desired a good return on his investment. The tax collector would often enroll other subordinate tax collectors who would not only help themselves to the taxes collected, but would pay a "surcharge" to their overseer. Because of the well-known nature of their methods, tax collectors were unusually despised in Jewish society.

Why do you eat and drink with tax collectors and "sinners"? This accusation by the Pharisees said as much about them as it did about Jesus. With very strict dietary and dining laws to consider, Pharisees tended to only eat with other Pharisees. This helped to avoid any issue of improper eating circumstances. The Pharisees also tended to view themselves as highly set apart. The thought of socializing with a despised tax collector or a common sinner would have repulsed them and threatened their haughty nature.

PRAYER AND PRAISE REPORT

Briefly share your prayer requests with the large group, making notations below. Then gather in small groups of two to four to pray for each other.

Date: _____

PRAYER REQUESTS

_____

_____

_____

_____

_____

_____

_____

_____

_____

_____

_____

_____

PRAISE REPORT

_____

_____

_____

_____

_____

_____

_____

_____

REFLECTIONS

Each day read the daily verse(s) and give prayerful consideration to what you learn about God, his Spirit, and his place in your life. Then record your thoughts, insights, or prayer in the Reflect section. On day six record a summary of what you have learned over the entire week through this study.

DAY 1   *"And Levi got up, left everything and followed him. Then Levi held a great banquet for Jesus at his house, and a large crowd of tax collectors and others were eating with them." (Luke 5:28–29)*

REFLECT: _____

_____

_____

_____

_____

_____

_____

_____

DAY 2   *"Suppose one of you has a hundred sheep and loses one of them. Does he not leave the ninety-nine in the open country and go after the lost sheep until he finds it? And when he finds it, he joyfully puts it on his shoulders and goes home. Then he calls his friends and neighbors together and says, 'Rejoice with me; I have found my lost sheep.'" (Luke 15:4–6)*

REFLECT: _____

_____

_____

_____

_____

_____

_____

DAY 3   *"Or suppose a woman has ten silver coins and loses one. Does she not light a lamp, sweep the house and search carefully until she finds it? And when she finds it, she calls her friends and neighbors together and says, 'Rejoice with me; I have found my lost coin.'"* (Luke 15:8–9)

REFLECT: _____

_____

_____

_____

_____

_____

_____

_____

_____

_____

_____

DAY 4   *"But the father said to his servants, 'Quick! Bring the best robe and put it on him. Put a ring on his finger and sandals on his feet. Bring the fattened calf and kill it. Let's have a feast and celebrate. For this son of mine was dead and is alive again; he was lost and is found.' So they began to celebrate."* (Luke 15:22–24)

REFLECT: _____

_____

_____

_____

_____

_____

_____

_____

_____

_____

_____

DAY 5   *"But in your hearts set apart Christ as Lord. Always be prepared to give an answer to everyone who asks you to give the reason for the hope that you have. But do this with gentleness and respect."* (1 Peter 3:15)

REFLECT: _____

_____

_____

_____

_____

_____

_____

_____

_____

_____

_____

_____

DAY 6   Use the following space to write any thoughts God has put in your heart and mind about the things discussed during session one and/or during your Reflections time this week.

SUMMARY: _____

_____

_____

_____

_____

_____

_____

_____

_____

_____

_____

_____

_____

SESSION 2
UNSTAINED INFLUENCE — DANIEL

Coleman Luck, a retired producer in Hollywood with a credible track record in television and film, lived and worked as a Christian in a field where Christians are rarely outspoken. One day, during the height of controversy over the movie *The Last Temptation of Christ*, he had a hard time getting to work. The movie, which many Protestants and Catholics found offensive to their faith, had aroused a culture war with many boycotting the movie and staging protests at Universal Studios where the movie was made. As it turned out, Universal Studios was also where Coleman Luck worked at the time producing a television series. But on this day, he wouldn't get to work because a crowd of two thousand angry Christians was blocking the driveway into the studio.

In the car with him that day was a fellow producer, with whom Coleman carpooled, who was not a believer. He looked at the crowd taunting them with John 3:16 signs, turned to Coleman Luck, and said, "You know, I would hate these people if it weren't for you."

What an incredible comment! This friend had so much respect for Coleman and his faith that he was willing to suspend judgment on other Christians who, quite honestly, were misbehaving. This story shows how powerful a statement one life can be, and how one friend in the right place is worth more than two thousand in the wrong.

CONNECTING WITH GOD'S FAMILY   15 MIN.

As Christians, we are called to engage with this world while acknowledging that our true citizenship is in heaven. But where do we draw the line? It can sometimes be difficult to know just how far we need to go. This week we'll look at the story of Daniel, a young Israelite who refused to compromise on his principles, and how God rewarded his stance.

1. Check in with your spiritual partner. Talk about how your quiet time went this week. Set and record a goal under the "WHAT is your next step for growth" question on your

Personal Health Plan on page 92. If you have time, discuss what you think are the differences between an opinion, a belief, and a conviction.

2. What one conviction do you hold so firmly that nothing could make you budge from it?

GROWING TO BE LIKE CHRIST   45–50 MIN.

Daniel was adamant. He would not eat that stuff! God had said no, and that settled it. Wasn't it bad enough that they had to live in captivity—did they have to break God's laws and eat food not fit for their bodies while they were at it? Because of their open faithfulness to God, Daniel and his friends remained hale and hearty over their ten-day, vegetable-and-water diet.

And then a strange thing happened—Daniel and his friends began to grow in status while in the king's service. Here they were, strangers in a strange land, and people were coming to them for answers. How could this be so? Daniel impressed King Nebuchadnezzar so much that the king actually praised Daniel's God (Daniel 2:47)!

Like Joseph before him, Daniel's faithfulness to God in a foreign land brought him notoriety, respect, and stature. That's his legacy! Daniel and his friends exerted leadership powerful enough to influence people groups to follow. How can we learn to live such uncompromising lives?

Read Daniel 1:8–21:

> But Daniel resolved not to defile himself with the royal food and wine, and he asked the chief official for permission not to defile himself this way. ⁹Now God had caused the official to show favor and sympathy to Daniel, ¹⁰but the official told Daniel, "I am afraid of my lord the king, who has assigned your food and drink. Why should he see you looking worse than the other young men your age? The king would then have my head because of you." ¹¹Daniel then said to the guard

whom the chief official had appointed over Daniel, Hana-niah, Mishael and Azariah, ¹²"Please test your servants for ten days: Give us nothing but vegetables to eat and water to drink. ¹³Then compare our appearance with that of the young men who eat the royal food, and treat your servants in accordance with what you see." ¹⁴So he agreed to this and tested them for ten days. ¹⁵At the end of the ten days they looked healthier and better nourished than any of the young men who ate the royal food. ¹⁶So the guard took away their choice food and the wine they were to drink and gave them vegetables instead. ¹⁷To these four young men God gave knowledge and understanding of all kinds of literature and learning. And Daniel could understand visions and dreams of all kinds. ¹⁸At the end of the time set by the king to bring them in, the chief official presented them to Nebuchadnezzar. ¹⁹The king talked with them, and he found none equal to Daniel, Hananiah, Mishael and Azariah; so they entered the king's service. ²⁰In every matter of wisdom and understanding about which the king questioned them, he found them ten times better than all the magicians and enchanters in his whole kingdom. ²¹And Daniel remained there until the first year of King Cyrus.

Read Daniel 2:46–48:

Then King Nebuchadnezzar fell prostrate before Daniel and paid him honor and ordered that an offering and incense be presented to him. ⁴⁷The king said to Daniel, "Surely your God is the God of gods and the Lord of kings and a revealer of mysteries, for you were able to reveal this mystery." ⁴⁸Then the king placed Daniel in a high position and lavished many gifts on him. He made him ruler over the entire province of Babylon and placed him in charge of all its wise men.

3. Consider Daniel's refusal to consume the royal food and wine, not knowing if anything else would be made available to him. What does this tell you about Daniel's devotion to his faith?

4. In order to avoid violating Mosaic law, Daniel first had to know what was in that law. How important is it for us as Christians today to know what is in God's Word? Why is it not enough to hear a sermon?

5. Read 1 Corinthians 6:12; 10:23–24. The Corinthian Christians knew they no longer lived under Mosaic laws and practices, and boasted of this freedom. Why do you think Paul advised caution in their choices?

6. What do you notice about the way Daniel behaved before the palace official? Was he rude or respectful? What difference do you think that ultimately made (Daniel 1:12–13)?

7. How did God reward Daniel's faithful choices? See Daniel 1:17, 19–20, and 2:48.

8. Have you ever turned down a more popular choice to do what you thought God wanted? Share the outcome of your story.

   What kind of reward should we expect for doing what is right?

9. Daniel became a very influential figure in Babylon and along with his friends exerted leadership so powerful that whole people groups were influenced to follow. Why is it important to live by our convictions?

10. Consider a few recent news headlines. What happens when a person fails to establish and live by a set of deeply held, personal convictions?

   How do convictions shape our character?

11. The book of Daniel is full of character-building lessons. One of the most stunning is found in Daniel 3, where Daniel's friends—Shadrach, Meshach, and Abednego—are ordered thrown into the fiery furnace for refusing to bow down and worship an idol made by King Nebuchadnezzar. Could they have rationalized it being okay to bow down for outward appearances while remaining committed to God in their hearts?

12. As a result of their faith, these three men emerged from the fire with their heads unsinged and there "was no smell of fire on them." How can we live in such a way that, though we go through fire, "not a hair of our heads is singed"?

FOR DEEPER STUDY

Read Daniel 1:6 – 7. King Nebuchadnezzar's chief palace official changed the names of Daniel and his friends:

- Daniel, which means "God is my judge" in Hebrew, was changed to Belteshazzar meaning "Bel, protect his life!" (Bel, also called Marduk, was the chief Babylonian god.)
- Hananiah, which means "the LORD shows grace," was changed to Shadrach, probably meaning "under the command of Aku" (the moon god).
- Mishael, which means "who is like God?", was changed to Meshach, probably meaning "who is like Aku?"
- Azariah, which means "the LORD helps," was changed to Abednego, meaning "servant of Negoebo" (or Nabu, the god of learning and writing).

What reasons might the king's official have had for changing Daniel's and his friends' names? What is the significance of the meaning of the names given them?

 DEVELOPING YOUR GIFTS TO SERVE OTHERS   10 MIN.

13. On pages 96 – 97 of this study guide you'll find the Personal Health Assessment. Take a few minutes right now to rate yourself in each area. You won't have to share your scores with the group.

Most people are as self-disciplined as they will ever be, left to themselves. That's sad, but true. The only way to become more disciplined is to find someone who will hold you accountable and help you become self-disciplined. For this study, that person is your spiritual partner.

Based on the results of your Health Assessment, about which area of your life are you feeling convicted and in need of more discipline to stay true? Is there something you could do to serve your small group and take a step in your area of conviction at the same time?

There are many ways group members can share the responsibilities involved in a successful small group. For instance, you could host the group in your home for a month, coordinate refreshments, help with prayer requests, track and recognize birthdays and anniversaries, plan a ministry project, or lead part of the discussion. What responsibility are you willing to assume for the next two or three months? Record who will host, who will lead, who will provide snacks, birthdays and anniversaries, and any ministry project plans on the Small Group Calendar on page 91.

14. As a group, begin planning a party to honor Jesus, like the one Matthew held, to which you will invite neighbors and friends who may not yet know Christ. Begin to think about how you will make him known to them through your witness. Set a date (the week following the last session of this study, perhaps), the place, and theme for your party now. Then ask someone to volunteer to bring invitations (or each person can supply their own if that works better for your group) to your group meeting next week. (See the Leader's Notes for more information and ideas.) Record your party date on the Small Group Calendar.

SHARING YOUR LIFE MISSION EVERY DAY   10 MIN.

15. Sit in circles of two to three people for this discussion. Turn to Telling Your Story on pages 98–99 of the Appendix and review the "How You Came to Know Christ" section. Begin to develop this part of your story by sharing within your circle. Make notes about this aspect of your story below and commit to writing it out this week.

One of our greatest fears is rejection. This may have been true for Daniel and his friends as well, but they didn't care if it cost them their lives; they were going to worship God. Daniel spent time every day talking with God, and he encouraged his friends to do the same (Daniel 2:18; 6:10). This gave them the strength they needed to persevere in their faith.

16. Have everyone answer the question: How can we pray for you this week? Write prayer requests on the Prayer and Praise Report provided on page 36. Close your time together by praying for the needs expressed today, remembering God's power is abundantly available to meet them. Also, commit to start praying daily for the party you are planning. Pray for the hearts of those you invite and for opportunities to share with them before, during, and after your party.

17. Use the Reflections verses at the end of this session in your quiet time this week. Record any thoughts or direction you receive from the Lord in the space provided.

STUDY NOTES

Not to defile himself with royal food and wine. There are many interpretations as to why Daniel resolved to abstain from royal food and wine. Some Bible commentators think that because this food more than likely came from the temple it would have been offered to a pagan deity. The vegetables, however, would have also been offered in the same manner. Others believe that royal food and wine as elements of celebration were not appropriate for the enslaved Israelites. By abstaining, Daniel and the others were demonstrating their state of grief and mourning. The avoidance of this royal food could also be as simple as honoring the practices of Jewish law in food preparation. Obviously, their captors would not practice Jewish rituals. Whatever the exact circumstance, Daniel and the others believed that by avoiding the royal food and wine, they would find God's favor. Indeed, they did.

Hananiah, Mishael, and Azariah. These are the Hebrew names for Daniel's three friends. The "chief official" gave them new names: Shadrach, Meshach, and Abednego. The name given to Daniel was Belteshazzar (Daniel 1:7).

Daniel could understand visions and dreams. For their obedience, Daniel and his friends are granted favor not only with the officials, but also with almighty God, who bestows on Daniel supernatural abilities to understand visions and dreams. As such, he's similar to Joseph who, having received these gifts in captivity (Genesis 40:8), also earned favor with his captors.

Until the first year of King Cyrus. The significance in this small verse is that Daniel survived seventy years of captivity under Nebuchadnezzar and now will see freedom and restoration. The rise of Cyrus brought about the return of God's people to their rightful possession, Israel's Promised Land (2 Chronicles 36:22–23; Ezra 1).

PRAYER AND PRAISE REPORT

Briefly share your prayer requests with the large group, making notations below. Then gather in small groups of two to four to pray for each other.

Date: _____

PRAYER REQUESTS

_____

_____

_____

_____

_____

_____

_____

_____

_____

_____

_____

_____

PRAISE REPORT

_____

_____

_____

_____

_____

_____

_____

_____

_____

REFLECTIONS

Each day read the daily verse(s) and give prayerful consideration to what you learn about God, his Spirit, and his place in your life. Then record your thoughts, insights, or prayer in the Reflect section. On day six record a summary of what you have learned over the entire week through this study.

DAY 1   " 'Everything is permissible for me' — but not everything is beneficial. 'Everything is permissible for me' — but I will not be mastered by anything." (1 Corinthians 6:12)

REFLECT: _____

_____

_____

_____

_____

_____

_____

_____

DAY 2   "And David shepherded them with integrity of heart; with skillful hands he led them." (Psalm 78:72)

REFLECT: _____

_____

_____

_____

_____

_____

_____

_____

DAY 3 *"Remain in me, and I will remain in you. No branch can bear fruit by itself; it must remain in the vine. Neither can you bear fruit unless you remain in me. I am the vine; you are the branches. If a man remains in me and I in him, he will bear much fruit; apart from me you can do nothing." (John 15:4–5)*

REFLECT: _____

_____

_____

_____

_____

_____

_____

_____

_____

_____

_____

DAY 4 *"Do you not know that in a race all the runners run, but only one gets the prize? Run in such a way as to get the prize." (1 Corinthians 9:24)*

REFLECT: _____

_____

_____

_____

_____

_____

_____

_____

_____

_____

DAY 5   *"What is more, I consider everything a loss compared to the surpassing greatness of knowing Christ Jesus my Lord, for whose sake I have lost all things. I consider them rubbish, that I may gain Christ."* (Philippians 3:8)

REFLECT: _____

_____

_____

_____

_____

_____

_____

_____

_____

_____

_____

_____

DAY 6   Use the following space to write any thoughts God has put in your heart and mind about the things discussed during session two and/or during your Reflections time this week.

SUMMARY: _____

_____

_____

_____

_____

_____

_____

_____

_____

_____

_____

UNITED INFLUENCE—
PETER AND CORNELIUS

My wife and I were having dinner out one night in a beach community in California. It was the Fourth of July and our favorite restaurants were full, so we decided to try a new place that had plenty of seats available. At the time, our third child was about ten months old and I had him strapped to my chest in one of those front-end carriers. The first thing I noticed was that this restaurant had no high chairs. That's unusual these days, especially in a place as progressive as California. Then the next thing I noticed explained why. As we watched people coming in, it finally dawned on us that we were in a gay restaurant.

Well, all this made me quite nervous, especially when our toddler started fussing, squealing, and covering himself (and me) with food. (I had to keep him in his kangaroo pouch just to contain him and that put him within reach of my plate.) My discomfort grew as I noticed two men looking over at our table quite a bit. I assumed they were offended by the rare occurrence of a child in their restaurant, and I entertained a few nasty thoughts about them in return, which, due to my prejudice, was relatively easy to do.

Overcome with uneasiness, I finished quickly and left my wife to close out the check. As I waited for her outside I could see that she had gone over to the table where the two men sat and spoke with them for a few minutes. When she finally joined us I asked her what that was all about.

"I went over to apologize for disrupting their dinner and they said, 'Oh no, quite the contrary. We love the sound of happy babies. You see, we are both retired physicians and for the last two years have been giving voluntary care to over six thousand abused babies. Hearing a happy child is like music to our ears.'"

I took the rebuke standing up, and was grateful for a good lesson in not passing judgment on anyone, especially those who are not of the household of faith.

CONNECTING WITH GOD'S FAMILY   20 MIN.

"But what about all those people who never hear about Jesus? What happens to them?" It's a question we've heard so much, we're

likely weary of it. It's easy to dismiss those who ask it, but perhaps they sincerely want to know. Is there an answer? God's Word tells us there is. In this session we'll read about a man who loved God and wanted to know more about him. Because he'd never heard about Jesus, God sent Peter to tell him about the Son who had made a way for man to be reconciled to God.

1. Go around the group and tell of a time you were stopped cold by a question you couldn't answer while sharing the gospel. What happened?

2. Pair up with your spiritual partner(s) and turn to your Personal Health Plan (pages 92–93). Share your progress in working on the goal you set for yourself last week. What obstacles hindered you from following through? Make a note about your partner's progress and how you can pray for him or her. Think about your beliefs before you were saved. What did you think about Christianity's requirement that we must believe in Christ to be saved?

GROWING TO BE LIKE CHRIST   40 MIN.

"I'm sure you all know," Peter began, a little stunned by the size of the crowd, "that it's against Jewish law for us to have anything to do with Gentiles."

They thought he would walk out, but Peter went on. "But God has been teaching me many new things lately, and one of them is that I no longer have the right to determine who or what is fit for God's service. Is that why you sent for me?"

Then Cornelius, a Roman centurion known for his love of God, told Peter about the vision he'd had just four days before, when a man in shining clothes told him God knew about his prayers and his heart to help the poor. He told him about how the man had directed him to get Peter and bring him to his home in Caesarea. He'd gone out into his neighborhood and, quietly so as not to arouse any suspicion, invited everyone he knew to come hear. And now they were here, awaiting Peter's every word.

Peter shook his head in amazement, recalling his own vision. This is what it meant! "What God has cleansed," he'd heard the Spirit say, "you are no longer to consider unholy." How could Jesus keep showing him so many new things, every day it seemed, when he wasn't even physically there anymore? Now here he was, stripping away years of prejudice to reach these people. God's love must be so much bigger than Peter could imagine.

"You know," Peter addressed the room, "all my life I believed God loved just one group of people. But now I see he loves them all. Anyone who fears God and wants to do what is right belongs to him." Peter proceeded to tell those gathered at Cornelius's house about Jesus, the man they had heard about, and how he was God's Son, sent to set captives free from the influence of the Devil. He said the news they'd heard about from Judea was true — Jesus did many great things, but in spite of them he had been crucified by jealous people who didn't understand.

Then he told them something they might not have heard — Jesus rose again on the third day! He told them that he, Peter, had known Jesus, had been taught by him, and had seen him after he was resurrected. He told them not everyone had seen Jesus, but only those God had chosen. And he told them that those God had chosen had also been commissioned to go and tell others about Jesus — the one long prophesied as the Savior and forgiver of sins.

Read Acts 10:27–43:

> *Talking with him, Peter went inside and found a large gathering of people.* [28]*He said to them: "You are well aware that it is against our law for a Jew to associate with a Gentile or visit him. But God has shown me that I should not call any man impure or unclean.* [29]*So when I was sent for, I came without raising any objection. May I ask why you sent for me?"* [30]*Cornelius answered: "Four days ago I was in my house praying at this hour, at three in the afternoon. Suddenly a man in shining clothes stood before me* [31]*and said, 'Cornelius, God has heard your prayer and remembered your gifts to the poor.* [32]*Send to Joppa for Simon who is called Peter. He is a guest in the home of Simon the tanner, who lives by the sea.'*

33So I sent for you immediately, and it was good of you to come. Now we are all here in the presence of God to listen to everything the Lord has commanded you to tell us." 34Then Peter began to speak: "I now realize how true it is that God does not show favoritism 35but accepts men from every nation who fear him and do what is right. 36You know the message God sent to the people of Israel, telling the good news of peace through Jesus Christ, who is Lord of all. 37You know what has happened throughout Judea, beginning in Galilee after the baptism that John preached—38how God anointed Jesus of Nazareth with the Holy Spirit and power, and how he went around doing good and healing all who were under the power of the devil, because God was with him. 39We are witnesses of everything he did in the country of the Jews and in Jerusalem. They killed him by hanging him on a tree, 40but God raised him from the dead on the third day and caused him to be seen. 41He was not seen by all the people, but by witnesses whom God had already chosen—by us who ate and drank with him after he rose from the dead. 42He commanded us to preach to the people and to testify that he is the one whom God appointed as judge of the living and the dead. 43All the prophets testify about him that everyone who believes in him receives forgiveness of sins through his name."

3. Peter began his address to the crowd gathered at Cornelius's home by declaring the laws of his Jewish faith, and then admitting God was changing his perspective. How important is this kind of transparency in sharing our faith with others, especially those with whom we may have had differences in the past?

4. In verses 30–32, what did Cornelius say to Peter that convinced him God was in this event?

5. One or two of you share times when you have clearly seen God's hand arranging circumstances in your lives. How did you know it was God?

6. What do you think God saw in Cornelius that prompted this answered prayer?

7. Now look at what Peter admits in verses 34–35. What does God want us to understand about how he sees people?

8. When it comes to sharing Christ with others, why do you think God wants us to see people through his eyes?

9. Peter's visit to Cornelius's home helped tear down the wall separating Jews and Gentiles. Salvation is available to *all* who call on the name of Christ. Do you think history would be different if Peter had disobeyed God in this moment and let his Jewish attitudes prevail? How?

   What does this say to you about the potential of any act of obedience on our part?

10. Talk about the character traits you see in Cornelius as revealed in this story. What about Peter's character?

FOR DEEPER STUDY

Read the rest of Acts 10, verses 44–48. What happened to those in the room while Peter was speaking? How does this further reassure us of God's power to save all who love him and desire to learn about him?

Compare God's words to David in 1 Samuel 16:7 with what he showed Peter in Acts 10:9–15. What similarities do you see?

DEVELOPING YOUR GIFTS TO SERVE OTHERS   10 MIN.

As a centurion, Cornelius was an influential man in his community of Caesarea. That influence obviously helped connect him with many people. We can see this in the relative ease with which he gathered a crowd in his home for Peter's arrival.

11. We each have a circle of influence in our own lives as well. Look at the Circles of Life diagram on page 19. Review the names listed there and add any new ones that come to mind. This is your party invitation list. Also, consider inviting Christian friends who are not part of your group. Write their names around the outside of the circles on your Circles of Life diagram.

If one person brought invitations for the whole group, pass out enough invitations to invite everyone on each person's list. If you have time, write the invitations now. If not, write them in the next day or two. Commit to delivering or mailing them this week.

SHARING YOUR LIFE MISSION EVERY DAY   10 MIN.

12. Acts 10:27 tells us Peter "went inside and found a large gathering of people." From what Scripture tells us (Acts 10:3–5, 30–32) Cornelius was nowhere specifically instructed to invite others. What does the fact he did invite others tell us about Cornelius?

13. Cornelius's attitude was conducive to sharing his faith with everyone he knew. In question 1 we talked about the questions and objections we receive that stop us from continuing to share our faith with someone. These questions/objections might include:

    • "I don't believe in God."
    • "I don't believe the Bible is God's Word."
    • "How can a loving God allow suffering?"

  How can we respond to these replies? Discuss the suggestions in Telling Your Story on page 99 of the appendix.

SURRENDERING YOUR LIFE FOR GOD'S PLEASURE   15–20 MIN.

14. Peter was amazed at how God kept expanding his thinking. Where have you been holding on to an old attitude God may want to change? Share your desire for God's work in your life with your group and pray for one another. Record your prayer requests on the Prayer and Praise Report on page 49. Plan to share in future weeks, as Peter did, how God is working in you to effect that change.

15. Use the Reflections verses at the end of this session in your quiet time this week. Record any thoughts or direction you receive from the Lord in the space provided.

STUDY NOTES

Against our law for a Jew to associate with a Gentile. Jews were not forbidden from associating with Gentiles, but the Gentiles' dietary practices made them ceremonially risky to associate with. Interestingly enough, the word used here for "associate with" is the same word used when Paul attempted to join the disciples in Jerusalem (Acts 9:26).

A man in shining clothes. According to Acts 10:3, an "angel of God" (messenger of God) appeared to Cornelius. How this revelation coincided with Peter's vision (10:10–11) further confirms that the messenger in this passage was not merely a man. Interestingly, the term "shining" or "radiant" used here is also used for the "bright" and morning star in Revelation 22:16.

God does not show favoritism. The idea of favoritism here, also interpreted "a respecter of persons," originates from the Greek word *prosopoleptes*, literally meaning "accepter of a face" and thus translated "exhibiting partiality." The root meaning betrays the superficiality of favoritism and reminds us of God's stance in 1 Samuel 16:7 "The LORD does not look at the things man looks at. Man looks at the outward appearance, but the LORD looks at the heart."

God ... caused him [Jesus] to be seen. He [Jesus] was not seen by all the people, but by witnesses whom God had already chosen. In the forty-day period following Jesus' resurrection, he revealed himself only to believers. Some of these witnesses became apostles. Peter reported that Jesus ate and drank with them following his resurrection (Luke 24:42–43). For further study, examine these reports: Luke 24:30–42; John 21:12–15; 1 Corinthians 15:4–8.

Briefly share your prayer requests with the large group, making notations below. Then gather in small groups of two to four to pray for each other.

Date: _____

PRAYER REQUESTS

_____

_____

_____

_____

_____

_____

_____

_____

_____

_____

_____

PRAISE REPORT

_____

_____

_____

_____

_____

_____

_____

_____

REFLECTIONS

Each day read the daily verse(s) and give prayerful consideration to what you learn about God, his Spirit, and his place in your life. Then record your thoughts, insights, or prayer in the Reflect section. On day six record a summary of what you have learned over the entire week through this study.

DAY 1   *"How good and pleasant it is when brothers live together in unity."*
(Psalm 133:1)

REFLECT: _____

_____

_____

_____

_____

_____

_____

_____

_____

DAY 2   *"Rejoice with those who rejoice; mourn with those who mourn. Live*
in harmony with one another. Do not be proud, but be willing to
associate with people of low position. Do not be conceited." (Romans
12:15 – 16)

REFLECT: _____

_____

_____

_____

_____

_____

_____

_____

_____

DAY 3   *"A new command I give you: Love one another. As I have loved you, so you must love one another. By this all men will know that you are my disciples, if you love one another." (John 13:34–35)*

REFLECT: _____

_____

_____

_____

_____

_____

_____

_____

_____

_____

DAY 4   *"Whatever happens, conduct yourselves in a manner worthy of the gospel of Christ. Then, whether I come and see you or only hear about you in my absence, I will know that you stand firm in one spirit, contending as one man for the faith of the gospel without being frightened in any way by those who oppose you. This is a sign to them that they will be destroyed, but that you will be saved—and that by God." (Philippians 1:27–28)*

REFLECT: _____

_____

_____

_____

_____

_____

_____

_____

_____

_____

DAY 5 *"As a prisoner for the Lord, then, I urge you to live a life worthy of the calling you have received. Be completely humble and gentle; be patient, bearing with one another in love. Make every effort to keep the unity of the Spirit through the bond of peace." (Ephesians 4:1–3)*

REFLECT: _____

_____

_____

_____

_____

_____

_____

_____

_____

_____

_____

_____

DAY 6 Use the following space to write any thoughts God has put in your heart and mind about the things discussed during session three and/ or during your Reflections time this week.

SUMMARY: _____

_____

_____

_____

_____

_____

_____

_____

_____

_____

REBORN INFLUENCE — NICODEMUS

It's not always easy to know where people are in their soul. Many keep their thoughts of God, life, and death to themselves, so don't ever think that you know what's going on in someone else's head or heart by what you see on the outside.

My daughter had a young man interested in her who came around often—sometimes a little too often for my comfort level. Especially when he appeared to be such a dark, brooding individual. Either there was something brewing in his head all the time or nothing at all. I even worried some about my daughter because I imagined he could be the personality type to hold everything inside until it exploded in some kind of violent behavior, and the fact that my daughter didn't give him any encouragement as to their relationship wasn't helping that impression. I even jokingly referred to him as the axe murderer. Until one time I had the chance to engage him in conversation, and another person emerged.

I found out his mind was working overtime, and it was working on some very vital issues as to faith, God, and the Bible. As soon as I hit that vein, I opened a mother lode of questions and opinions and we talked openly for some time about things of God. It was soon obvious that our conversation and his observation of our lives was making a profound impact on his own journey of faith.

CONNECTING WITH GOD'S FAMILY   20 MIN.

Sometimes the crowd we associate with can hold us back from discovering real life in Christ. Afraid of what others might think, or unwilling to face their disapproval, we hold back, ultimately cheating ourselves. In this session, we'll look at the story of Nicodemus, an influential Pharisee and member of the Sanhedrin. Because he valued understanding Jesus' teaching, he came to him—secretly, likely afraid of being seen by his colleagues—to receive clarification. His fear of his colleagues turned to the joy of salvation over time. Today, this serves as an example of how to find new life in Christ (John 3:3, 15), and we have a glimpse into the heart that drove God to send Jesus into the world to save us (3:16).

1. Share a time — even from your school days — when peer pressure kept you from something you really wanted to do or know more about. How did you feel about it later?

2. Check in with your spiritual partner(s), or with another partner if yours is absent. Share something God taught you during your time in his Word this week, or read a brief section from your journal. Be sure to write down your partner's progress on page 93.

GROWING TO BE LIKE CHRIST   40 MIN.

Nicodemus had heard the things Jesus was saying, and he was intrigued. What did he mean about being reborn? Yes, he knew how his colleagues on the Sanhedrin felt about this man. He knew they didn't trust him, even thought he was sent from the Devil to mislead them. But Nicodemus wasn't sure. There was something about this man. What was it? He had to know. After all, Nicodemus was no longer young. If there was more to learn about entering the kingdom of heaven than he already knew, now was the time to find out.

So he went to Jesus by night, hoping for a chance to get to know this rabbi better. He marveled at the things Jesus told him.

"People give birth to human bodies," Jesus said, "but the spirit can only be brought to life by God's Spirit."

How could these things Jesus was saying be true? Jesus wanted Nicodemus to understand that knowledge isn't everything. To be saved, you must understand God, recognize the depth of his love, and take hold of the free gift he offers.

Read John 3:1–21:

> Now there was a man of the Pharisees named Nicodemus,
> a member of the Jewish ruling council. ²He came to Jesus at
> night and said, "Rabbi, we know you are a teacher who has
> come from God. For no one could perform the miraculous
> signs you are doing if God were not with him." ³In reply Jesus

declared, "I tell you the truth, no one can see the kingdom of God unless he is born again." [4]"How can a man be born when he is old?" Nicodemus asked. "Surely he cannot enter a second time into his mother's womb to be born!" [5]Jesus answered, "I tell you the truth, no one can enter the kingdom of God unless he is born of water and the Spirit. [6]Flesh gives birth to flesh, but the Spirit gives birth to spirit. [7]You should not be surprised at my saying, 'You must be born again.' [8]The wind blows wherever it pleases. You hear its sound, but you cannot tell where it comes from or where it is going. So it is with everyone born of the Spirit." [9]"How can this be?" Nicodemus asked. [10]"You are Israel's teacher," said Jesus, "and do you not understand these things? [11]I tell you the truth, we speak of what we know, and we testify to what we have seen, but still you people do not accept our testimony. [12]I have spoken to you of earthly things and you do not believe; how then will you believe if I speak of heavenly things? [13]No one has ever gone into heaven except the one who came from heaven—the Son of Man. [14]Just as Moses lifted up the snake in the desert, so the Son of Man must be lifted up, [15]that everyone who believes in him may have eternal life. [16]For God so loved the world that he gave his one and only Son, that whoever believes in him shall not perish but have eternal life. [17]For God did not send his Son into the world to condemn the world, but to save the world through him. [18]Whoever believes in him is not condemned, but whoever does not believe stands condemned already because he has not believed in the name of God's one and only Son. [19]This is the verdict: Light has come into the world, but men loved darkness instead of light because their deeds were evil. [20]Everyone who does evil hates the light, and will not come into the light for fear that his deeds will be exposed. [21]But whoever lives by the truth comes into the light, so that it may be seen plainly that what he has done has been done through God."

3. Nicodemus was a wealthy and influential man. What does it say to you about his character that he went to Jesus, even though he knew what his friends/colleagues would think if they knew?

4. What does Nicodemus's story teach us? What must we each do with the Son of God?

5. In verse 2 Nicodemus said to Jesus, "No one could perform the miraculous signs you are doing if God were not with him." Why do you think Nicodemus could see that about Jesus when his Sanhedrin brethren could not?

6. From verses 3–7, what does it mean to you to be born again? Is it enough to live a good life? If you have any uncertainties about this passage, discussing it in your group is a great way to settle those questions.

7. In verse 8, Jesus compared the work of the Spirit to the wind. We can't control our physical birth, but can we control the work of the Spirit? Explain your answer.

8. It's been said by scholars that the Old Testament is Christ concealed and the New Testament is Christ revealed. What do you think Jesus wanted Nicodemus to fully understand by his words to him in verses 10–13? It is the lack of this understanding that keeps many Jews from seeing their Messiah even today.

9. In verse 14, Jesus refers to God making a way for the Israelites to repent and come to him. (See also Numbers 21:6–9.) What do you think Jesus means when he says he must be lifted up?

What do you think is the symbolism represented in verse 14?

What must we do to be saved?

10. In verse 17, Jesus tells us he was not sent to the world to condemn it. As Christ-followers, how does this verse speak to us regarding our attitudes toward others?

What *does* condemn a person? See verse 18.

11. This passage is full of so much rich teaching from Jesus — every verse a nugget. Look over verses 20–21 and spend a few minutes discussing where you see evidence today of the truths represented by Jesus' words. Think about what coming into the light versus hiding from the light says about our character.

FOR DEEPER STUDY

Read more about Nicodemus:

- In John 7:45–52, he spoke up for Christ. How did he do it?

- In John 19:39–40, he honored Christ. What did he do?

It's interesting to note that Nicodemus is often referred to as "the one who came to Jesus by night." Why do you think he approached Jesus that way?

DEVELOPING YOUR GIFTS TO SERVE OTHERS   10 MIN.

12. Nicodemus recognized the gift of teaching Jesus possessed. Do you have a gift that causes others to seek you out? Even if you are already using that ability to bless others, look for new opportunities to share his love through your giftedness.

13. Take some time now to discuss what is next for your group. Will you be staying together for another study? What will your next study be? Turn to the Small Group Agreement on pages 89–90 and talk about any changes you would like to make as you move forward.

SHARING YOUR LIFE MISSION EVERY DAY   15–20 MIN.

14. John 3:16 is probably one of the most familiar verses in Scripture to the Christian. With familiarity often comes a sense of ordinariness, but in reality, this is one of the most extraordinary truths of all time. Let's spend a few moments reviewing what it says:

- Who does God love?

- Is anyone excluded from God's love?

- What did God give because of his love?

- Who did God give him for?

- What is God's promise and what must we do to receive it?

- *Who do you need to tell?*

15. Separate into subgroups of two or three people for this discussion. Turn to Telling Your Story on pages 98–99 of the appendix and review "The Difference Christ Has Made in Your Life" section. Share the highlights of this part of your story within your circle. Make notes about this aspect of your story below and commit to writing it out this week.

 SURRENDERING YOUR LIFE FOR GOD'S PLEASURE   10 MIN.

16. Nicodemus apparently initially became a secret believer, but his heart was revealed over time. Are you keeping your faith a secret from anyone? Share your burden with your group and share any other prayer requests with the group. Share any praises as well. Write down prayer requests and praises on the Prayer and Praise Report provided on page 61. As God answers these requests, be sure to celebrate how he is working among and through your group.

17. Use the Reflections verses at the end of this session in your quiet time this week. Record any thoughts or direction you receive from the Lord in the space provided.

STUDY NOTES

Pharisees. This major sect of Judaism taught that only the most righteous would experience immortality. To achieve this, the Pharisees taught a strict observance of the Law and a complete separation from the heathen. The name *Pharisee* actually means "separatist," though its original meaning had more to do with separating from the heathen during captivity in the time of Zerubbabel and Ezra. This stance of separation caused a great deal of conflict with Jesus' teaching and practices of interacting and socializing with "sinners."

Jewish ruling council. John uses this term more than likely to indicate that Nicodemus was a member of the Sanhedrin. This ruling council was made up of high priests, members of privileged families, elders, and scribes. There were seventy members of the Sanhedrin. Membership was for life, and new members were appointed by existing members. Officially, the Sanhedrin had authority only over Judea and had no formal authority over Jesus. Practically, the Sanhedrin's rulings were felt throughout the Jewish world.

Born of water and the Spirit. This passage has been subjected to a variety of interpretations. Some have taken this phrase to mean that one must be physically born (water), then spiritually born (Spirit) to be saved. Others have taken this phrase to mean that one must be saved and baptized (water), then later filled with the Spirit. Another common understanding is that the baptism of water signifies purity, which might indicate the baptism of repentance. "Born of … the Spirit" would, then, indicate a spiritual birth or salvation. While the first explanation involving physical birth and spiritual birth may seem simplistic, the next statement by Jesus seems to lean toward this explanation: "Flesh gives birth to flesh, but the Spirit gives birth to spirit" (John 3:6). Nicodemus seems a bit perplexed, "How can this be?" (3:9) indicating that he is trying to comprehend this second birth.

Moses lifted up the snake in the desert. This is a reference to Numbers 21 when the Lord sent venomous snakes to punish the complaining Israelite people. Many died. When the people repented of their complaining and unbelief (Numbers 21:7), God made a provision for them: "Make a snake and put it up on a pole; anyone who is bitten can look at it and live" (21:8). The bronze snake is a clear and obvious symbol of Jesus being raised up at Calvary (John 3:14).

Briefly share your prayer requests with the large group, making notations below. Then gather in small groups of two to four to pray for each other.

Date: _____

PRAYER REQUESTS

_____

_____

_____

_____

_____

_____

_____

_____

_____

_____

_____

PRAISE REPORT

_____

_____

_____

_____

_____

_____

_____

_____

REFLECTIONS

Each day read the daily verse(s) and give prayerful consideration to what you learn about God, his Spirit, and his place in your life. Then record your thoughts, insights, or prayer in the Reflect section. On day six record a summary of what you have learned over the entire week through this study.

DAY 1   *"In reply Jesus declared, 'I tell you the truth, no one can see the kingdom of God unless he is born again.' "(John 3:3)*

REFLECT: _____

_____

_____

_____

_____

_____

_____

_____

_____

_____

DAY 2   *"Jesus answered, 'I tell you the truth, no one can enter the kingdom of God unless he is born of water and the Spirit. Flesh gives birth to flesh, but the Spirit gives birth to spirit.' " (John 3:5–6)*

REFLECT: _____

_____

_____

_____

_____

_____

_____

_____

_____

DAY 3   *"Just as Moses lifted up the snake in the desert, so the Son of Man must be lifted up, that everyone who believes in him may have eternal life." (John 3:14–15)*

REFLECT: _____

_____

_____

_____

_____

_____

_____

_____

_____

_____

_____

DAY 4   *"For God so loved the world that he gave his one and only Son, that whoever believes in him shall not perish but have eternal life. For God did not send his Son into the world to condemn the world, but to save the world through him. Whoever believes in him is not condemned, but whoever does not believe stands condemned already because he has not believed in the name of God's one and only Son." (John 3:16–18)*

REFLECT: _____

_____

_____

_____

_____

_____

_____

_____

_____

DAY 5 *"So we have stopped evaluating others from a human point of view. At one time we thought of Christ merely from a human point of view. How differently we know him now! This means that anyone who belongs to Christ has become a new person. The old life is gone; a new life has begun!" (2 Corinthians 5:16–17 NLT)*

REFLECT: _____

_____

_____

_____

_____

_____

_____

_____

_____

_____

_____

_____

DAY 6 Use the following space to write any thoughts God has put in your heart and mind about the things discussed during session four and/or during your Reflections time this week.

SUMMARY: _____

_____

_____

_____

_____

_____

_____

_____

_____

_____

BROTHERLY INFLUENCE—ANDREW AND PETER

There's nothing more exciting than a brand-new believer. My wife became a Christian four years before I met her. She was a flight attendant at the time. Her zeal to introduce others to Jesus was reminiscent of the woman at the well who ran and got the whole town out to see Jesus.

My wife immediately began an international organization of Christian flight attendants for fellowship and for reaching out to others in their profession. She organized events where many people came to Christ, and bid for trips with another flight attendant who was a Christian so they could witness on the planes. They even bid for the shorter trips so they could talk to as many different people as possible. They had two goals for every flight: to talk to at least one person about Christ, and to be encouraged by at least one person who already knew him. God met those requests every time.

In her zeal, however, she went home to her family over the holidays and vacations and had little or no success. Later she would realize that she pressed them too hard. Jesus said a prophet is without honor in his own town, and I think the same goes for family. That's because members of your family think they know you and are more likely to ignore changes, choosing instead to see you as they've always seen you. "Isn't this the carpenter's son—the son of Joseph?" they said of Jesus. "Don't we know this guy?"

With family members you have to walk openly and be patient. Change takes time. And remember, we don't save anyone. We just introduce them to Jesus through telling our own story. God does the rest.

CONNECTING WITH GOD'S FAMILY   20 MIN.

Sharing Christ with friends or family members can sometimes seem daunting or make us feel uncomfortable. *What if I say the wrong thing? What if they don't want to hear?* But as we learn from the example of Andrew in this session, we are simply to be Jesus' witnesses, offering the evidence of what he has done in our lives.

1. Do you have a brother or sister who has been especially influential in your life? Briefly share a story about that influence.

2. Sit with your spiritual partner(s). Share a time when fear of saying the wrong thing kept you from speaking up. What kind of impact, if any, did last week's discussion about "The Difference Christ Has Made in Your Life" have on your week?

GROWING TO BE LIKE CHRIST   40 MIN.

For some time now, Andrew had been listening to John the Baptist. Those things he'd been saying about being a voice in the wilderness, clearing the way for the Lord's coming, excited him. *Is the Lord coming? Oh, we have waited so long!* So today, after their fishing was done, the nets hauled in, and the boat back in its dock, he'd come back to meet with his teacher at the Jordan River.

They were standing together—Andrew, John the Baptist, and another of John's disciples—when Jesus passed by. *Wasn't that the guy? The one they'd been hearing about? The one John baptized just yesterday?* They had to find out, so Andrew and his companion followed Jesus.

"What do you want?" Jesus asked them. So they asked where he was staying and Jesus took them along, where they spent the rest of the day together.

Andrew had heard what John said about this man. Now he saw for himself. *Simon will be so excited,* Andrew thought, as he hurried home to get his brother. *The Messiah is really here!*

When Andrew returned with Simon, both brothers were astounded by what Jesus said. He looked at Simon as if he knew him, and said, "You are Simon, the son of John. But from now on you'll be called Peter." What did it all mean?

Read John 1:35–42:

> *The next day John was there again with two of his disciples.*
> *36When he saw Jesus passing by, he said, "Look, the Lamb of God!" 37When the two disciples heard him say this, they followed Jesus. 38Turning around, Jesus saw them following and asked, "What do you want?" They said, "Rabbi" (which means Teacher), "where are you staying?" 39"Come," he replied, "and you will see." So they went and saw where he was staying, and spent that day with him. It was about the tenth hour. 40Andrew, Simon Peter's brother, was one of the*

two who heard what John had said and who had followed Jesus. *41*The first thing Andrew did was to find his brother Simon and tell him, "We have found the Messiah" (that is, the Christ). *42*And he brought him to Jesus. Jesus looked at him and said, "You are Simon son of John. You will be called Cephas" (which, when translated, is Peter).

3. How did Andrew learn about Jesus? See John 1:35–37.

4. What did Andrew do when he saw Jesus walking by (verses 37–39)?

5. Why do you think these disciples were willing to leave John the Baptist to follow Jesus?

6. Jesus asked Andrew and the other disciple (many scholars believe this was John, who would later become one of the twelve apostles) what they wanted. Why do you think this matters to Jesus?

What do *you* seek?

7. What does it say about the character of someone to want to share life-changing news with another? Is it easier, or harder, to share Christ with a family member? Why?

8. What is the first thing Andrew did after meeting Jesus? See verses 41 – 42.

9. The disciples used several names in referring to Jesus in this passage. In verse 36, John calls him "Lamb of God"; in verse 38, he is called "Rabbi"; and in verse 41 they call him "Messiah." A few verses later (John 1:49), he's called "Son of God" and "King of Israel." How does our view of someone, including Jesus, change as we get to know them better?

10. When Jesus met Simon, he immediately changed his name to Peter, which means "rock." We don't know what Peter was like before this moment, and while he walked with Jesus he was unstable at best. But we know that in the early days of the church, Peter became a rock-solid figure. How can a new identity influence our character?

FOR DEEPER STUDY

Three times in Scripture Andrew is described introducing people to Jesus: to his brother Simon (John 1:41 – 42), the boy with the fish and loaves (6:8 – 9), and some Greeks (12:20 – 22). Why do you think these stories were told in the Bible?

To learn more about Andrew's character, read the following verses:

- Matthew 4:18 – 20; 10:2
- Mark 13:3 – 4
- John 6:8 – 9; 12:21 – 22

What kind of man do you think this apostle was?

DEVELOPING YOUR GIFTS TO SERVE OTHERS   10 MIN.

11. Andrew and Peter were both fishermen, but that's not how most of us think of them. A vocation is one thing — it's what we do to put fish on the table. But gifts are often found in those places that make our heart beat a little faster. For Andrew, it was learning from Jesus. For Peter, it would become a life mission. What do you love to do so much you find time to do it, even when your schedule is completely full? How could that love be turned into a ministry?

12. In session four (pages 57–58) we talked about using our gifts effectively. In what ways have you seen that you can use your gifts to serve others?

13. Finalize your party plans before closing your meeting today. Think about the role each of you could take in making the party a success for everyone. Some ideas include being a greeter or host/hostess, setting up and playing music, making name tags, arranging for food, purchasing or making take-away gifts for attendees, and so on.

SHARING YOUR LIFE MISSION EVERY DAY   10 MIN.

14. As a group, review Telling Your Story. Share which part of your story is the most difficult for you to tell. Which is the easiest for you? If you have time, a few of you share your story with the group.

15. Spend some time praying for your party, for the people you have invited, and for each other. Record prayer requests on the Prayer and Praise Report provided on page 71. Have any of last session's prayers been answered? If so, celebrate these responses from God.

16. The scene described in John 1:35–42 has earned Andrew the posthumous title of "first missionary." Andrew shows us that sharing Christ is the natural overflow of a joyful heart. Using the Reflections verses at the end of this session, make a date with Jesus this week and spend some time soaking in his presence. Then watch what happens as a result!

STUDY NOTES

John ... with two of his disciples. The account begins with John the Baptist and two of his disciples. John 1:40 reveals that one of the disciples was Andrew, Simon Peter's brother. It is commonly held that the other disciple was the "beloved disciple" or John, who recorded this account. Some believe that this second disciple might have been Philip instead.

The tenth hour. The tenth hour from sunrise, according to the Roman calculation of time, would have been four in the afternoon.

Simon son of John. You will be called Cephas. Jesus knew not only who Simon was, but also who he would become. Cephas is the Aramaic for Peter, a Greek name meaning "rock." This name is appropriate in light of Matthew 16:18 where Jesus proclaims, "You are Peter, and on this rock I will build my church." It should be noted that Jesus was not speaking of building the church on Peter per se, but rather on Peter's proclamation: "You are the Christ, the Son of the living God" (16:16).

Briefly share your prayer requests with the large group, making notations below. Then gather in small groups of two to four to pray for each other.

Date: _____

PRAYER REQUESTS

_____
_____
_____
_____
_____
_____
_____
_____
_____
_____
_____
_____

PRAISE REPORT

_____
_____
_____
_____
_____
_____
_____
_____
_____

REFLECTIONS

Each day read the daily verse(s) and give prayerful consideration to what you learn about God, his Spirit, and his place in your life. Then record your thoughts, insights, or prayer in the Reflect section. On day six record a summary of what you have learned over the entire week through this study.

DAY 1   *"For, 'Everyone who calls on the name of the Lord will be saved.' How, then, can they call on the one they have not believed in? And how can they believe in the one of whom they have not heard? And how can they hear without someone preaching to them?" (Romans 10:13–14)*

REFLECT: _____

_____

_____

_____

_____

_____

_____

_____

DAY 2   *"As Jesus was walking beside the Sea of Galilee, he saw two brothers, Simon called Peter and his brother Andrew. They were casting a net into the lake, for they were fishermen. 'Come, follow me,' Jesus said, 'and I will make you fishers of men.' At once they left their nets and followed him." (Matthew 4:18–20)*

REFLECT: _____

_____

_____

_____

_____

_____

DAY 3   *"Going on from there, he saw two other brothers, James son of Zebedee and his brother John. They were in a boat with their father Zebedee, preparing their nets. Jesus called them, and immediately they left the boat and their father and followed him." (Matthew 4:21–22)*

REFLECT: _____

_____

_____

_____

_____

_____

_____

_____

_____

_____

DAY 4   *"Peter said to him, 'We have left everything to follow you!' 'I tell you the truth,' Jesus replied, 'no one who has left home or brothers or sisters or mother or father or children or fields for me and the gospel will fail to receive a hundred times as much in this present age (homes, brothers, sisters, mothers, children and fields—and with them, persecutions) and in the age to come, eternal life.'" (Mark 10:28–30)*

REFLECT: _____

_____

_____

_____

_____

_____

_____

_____

_____

_____

DAY 5   *"And we also thank God continually because, when you received the word of God, which you heard from us, you accepted it not as the word of men, but as it actually is, the word of God, which is at work in you who believe." (1 Thessalonians 2:13)*

REFLECT: _____

_____

_____

_____

_____

_____

_____

_____

_____

_____

_____

_____

DAY 6   Use the following space to write any thoughts God has put in your heart and mind about the things discussed during session five and/or during your Reflections time this week.

SUMMARY: _____

_____

_____

_____

_____

_____

_____

_____

_____

_____

_____

ALIEN INFLUENCE—
PAUL AND THE GENTILES AT ATHENS

One of the most important things about sharing with people you don't know is to find common ground. You'll find out pretty quickly whether or not they might be open to talking about Christ. This isn't being ashamed of the gospel; it is caring about someone enough to listen to them first. Find out what they want to talk about instead of insisting that they listen to what we want to talk about.

Like the guy who bought one of those witnessing T-shirts at a Christian store and thought he'd get a chance to witness wearing it. After wearing it on a number of occasions when he was out and about, he came to the conclusion that the witnessing T-shirt didn't work.

Then one day he came home after riding on the bus doing errands all over town and realized he had gotten into a number of conversations that day, one of which had opened into a wonderful opportunity to share his faith and introduce someone to Christ. That's when he realized he was not wearing his witnessing T-shirt, but his Fender guitar T-shirt.

He found common ground. He connected with other guitar players. His interest opened up a chance to engage others with the same interest, and his conversations naturally moved to what was important to him. His conclusion? The Fender guitar T-shirt witnesses better than the witnessing T-shirt!

CONNECTING WITH GOD'S FAMILY   20 MIN.

Throughout this study, we've examined many ways to influence others for Christ—from reaching others as Jesus did, to refusing to compromise, to recognizing the importance of tearing down the walls that separate us. We've looked at the need to reach out for the truth while there is still time and discussed sharing Christ from the overflow of our own joy. In this session we'll learn from a master teacher, as we see how Paul himself took advantage of an unexpected opportunity and brought the gospel message to a people who had never heard of the one true God. We can't know where our witness will have the most influence—but like Paul, we can always be ready to make an impact for Christ. Sooner or later, most of us are in a position of either delivering or receiving major news for the first time — no journalism degree required.

1. Think of when you first heard about Christ. How did you take the news? Were you skeptical? How did you verify what you heard?

2. Turn to your Personal Health Plan (pages 92 – 93). Share with your spiritual partner(s) how your time with God went this week. What is one thing you discovered? Or, what obstacles hindered you from following through? How is your progress in the goal you set for yourself in this study? Make a note about your partner's progress and how you can continue to pray for him or her.

GROWING TO BE LIKE CHRIST   40 MIN.

If there was one thing you could say about the apostle Paul, it's that he didn't miss an opportunity. During his church-planting travels, Paul was on a layover in Athens waiting for Silas and Timothy to join him. Now the reason they weren't together was that Paul had fled Thessalonica to Berea, only to find out his enemies had followed him there as well. So he'd escaped and was laying low in Athens — but not for long.

While there, Paul took in the sights, and found them both beautiful and disturbing. Idols as far as the eye could see. So Paul, being Paul, sought an opportunity to engage the thinkers of Athens in conversation. What better place than the Areopagus, or Mars Hill, where the council, or court of justice, gathered?

The Greeks were idolatrous, but eager to hear new points of view, so in addition to listening to him daily in the public square, they welcomed Paul to their meeting.

Paul began his message by pointing to what he and his listeners had in common — they were all lovers of God. But to the Greeks, God was unknown. Rather than delivering a recital of a history that would have been meaningless to them, Paul picked up on their obvious belief and used it as the arrow to drive them to the one true God.

Read Acts 17:22–34:

> Paul then stood up in the meeting of the Areopagus and said: "Men of Athens! I see that in every way you are very religious. [23]For as I walked around and looked carefully at your objects of worship, I even found an altar with this inscription: TO AN UNKNOWN GOD. Now what you worship as something unknown I am going to proclaim to you. [24]The God who made the world and everything in it is the Lord of heaven and earth and does not live in temples built by hands. [25]And he is not served by human hands, as if he needed anything, because he himself gives all men life and breath and everything else. [26]From one man he made every nation of men, that they should inhabit the whole earth; and he determined the times set for them and the exact places where they should live. [27]God did this so that men would seek him and perhaps reach out for him and find him, though he is not far from each one of us. [28]'For in him we live and move and have our being.' As some of your own poets have said, 'We are his offspring.' [29]Therefore since we are God's offspring, we should not think that the divine being is like gold or silver or stone—an image made by man's design and skill. [30]In the past God overlooked such ignorance, but now he commands all people everywhere to repent. [31]For he has set a day when he will judge the world with justice by the man he has appointed. He has given proof of this to all men by raising him from the dead." [32]When they heard about the resurrection of the dead, some of them sneered, but others said, "We want to hear you again on this subject." [33]At that, Paul left the Council. [34]A few men became followers of Paul and believed. Among them was Dionysius, a member of the Areopagus, also a woman named Damaris, and a number of others.

3. Paul began his message with a statement everyone present could agree on (verse 22). What does this indicate about Paul's strategy for sharing Christ with these people?

4. In verse 23, what was Paul promising to make known to the Greeks?

5. Why do you think he mentioned temples in verse 24?

6. As a rabbi in the Jewish faith, Paul had been well taught by Gamaliel, a leading Jewish scholar, and had spent many years studying the Scriptures. This uniquely prepared him to speak to this group. What evidence do you find of his preparation in verses 24 – 26? Why do you think preparation is important?

7. On Mars Hill, Paul delivered a message so eloquent, one might expect that the whole crowd would have been won over. What do we learn about the reaction to his message from verses 32 – 34?

8. Read Matthew 13:3 – 9 or Luke 8:4 – 15. How does Jesus prepare us, through these verses, for the reactions we'll encounter when the gospel message is shared?

9. How important is it that our witness for Christ always be well received? Note that souls were added to God's kingdom at Mars Hill. Read Paul's words in 1 Corinthians 3:5 – 8. What do these verses tell us about our part in doing God's work?

10. Read 1 Timothy 2:1–4 and 2 Peter 3:9. What assurance do we have from God that our witness for him is never unproductive?

FOR DEEPER STUDY

Read Colossians 4:2–6, where Paul offers advice for preparing ourselves to deal with those outside the faith. We are, above all, to devote ourselves to prayer.

- For what are we to be watchful and thankful (verse 2)?

- What is the "mystery," or "secret," of Christ that Paul refers to in verse 3?

- Paul requests prayer for clarity in verse 4. What does he need clarity about?

- According to verses 5–6, what is Paul's counsel for our behavior toward outsiders? Why is this critical?

DEVELOPING YOUR GIFTS TO SERVE OTHERS   20 MIN.

Paul was a gifted orator, so sharing Christ came naturally for him. That is not true for all of us, but sooner or later each one of us will be asked to speak up for Christ.

11. Throughout this study we have had the opportunity to develop our individual testimonies. One way your group can serve each other is to provide a safe forum to "practice" telling our stories. In the last session you began sharing your complete testimonies with each other. Continue to take turns sharing your testimonies now. Set a time limit—say two to three minutes each. Don't miss this great opportunity to get to know one another better and encourage each other's growth too.

12. If your group still needs to make decisions about continuing to meet after this last session, have that discussion now. Review your Small Group Agreement on pages 89–90 and evaluate how well you met your goals and discuss any changes you want to make as you move forward. Talk about what you will study, who will lead, and where and when you will meet.

SURRENDERING YOUR LIFE FOR GOD'S PLEASURE   15–20 MIN.

13. Share with your group one thing you would like God to do in your life as a result of this study. Record your prayer requests on the Prayer and Praise Report on page 81.

14. Use the Reflections verses at the end of this session in your quiet time this week. Record any thoughts or direction you receive from the Lord in the space provided.

15. Have a great party and come back to your next study refreshed!

STUDY NOTES

Areopagus. The Areopagus or "hill of Ares" is the Greek equivalent of the Roman god, Mars. Thus, the Areopagus is also known as Mars Hill.

Your own poets. One of the poets Paul mentions here is Epimenides the Cretan. Paul quotes from the fourth line of a quatrain:

> They fashioned a tomb for thee, O holy and high one —
> The Cretans, always liars, evil beasts, idle bellies!
> But thou art not dead; thou livest and abidest for ever;
> For in thee we live and move and have our being.

"The other part is the fifth line of the Phainomena of Paul's fellow-Cilician Artus, which opens with the words, 'Let us begin with Zeus. Never, O men, let us leave him unmentioned ... all ways are full of Zeus and all meeting places of men; the sea and the harbors are full of him. In every direction we all have to do with Zeus; for we are also his offspring" (*The Book of Acts*, F. F. Bruce, The New International Commentary on the New Testament. Grand Rapids, Mich.: Eerdmans, 1984, 359–360).

While the Athenians had a basic concept of God, their mythology assigned these attributes to the wrong deity. Paul picks up on their understanding and sense of God, then directs them to the one true God.

Briefly share your prayer requests with the large group, making notations below. Then gather in small groups of two to four to pray for each other.

Date: _____

PRAYER REQUESTS

_____
_____
_____
_____
_____
_____
_____
_____
_____
_____
_____
_____

PRAISE REPORT

_____
_____
_____
_____
_____
_____
_____
_____
_____

REFLECTIONS

Each day read the daily verse(s) and give prayerful consideration to what you learn about God, his Spirit, and his place in your life. Then record your thoughts, insights, or prayer in the Reflect section. On day six record a summary of what you have learned over the entire week through this study.

DAY 1   *"I urge, then, first of all, that requests, prayers, intercession and thanks-giving be made for everyone—for kings and all those in authority, that we may live peaceful and quiet lives in all godliness and holiness. This is good, and pleases God our Savior, who wants all men to be saved and to come to a knowledge of the truth." (1 Timothy 2:1–4)*

REFLECT: _____

_____

_____

_____

_____

_____

_____

_____

DAY 2   *"The Lord is not slow in keeping his promise, as some understand slowness. He is patient with you, not wanting anyone to perish, but everyone to come to repentance." (2 Peter 3:9)*

REFLECT: _____

_____

_____

_____

_____

_____

_____

_____

DAY 3   *"By the grace God has given me, I laid a foundation as an expert builder, and someone else is building on it. But each one should be careful how he builds." (1 Corinthians 3:10)*

REFLECT: _____

_____

_____

_____

_____

_____

_____

_____

_____

_____

_____

DAY 4   *"Then Jesus came to them and said, 'All authority in heaven and on earth has been given to me. Therefore go and make disciples of all nations, baptizing them in the name of the Father and of the Son and of the Holy Spirit, and teaching them to obey everything I have commanded you. And surely I am with you always, to the very end of the age.'" (Matthew 28:18–20)*

REFLECT: _____

_____

_____

_____

_____

_____

_____

_____

_____

_____

DAY 5 *"But you are a chosen people, a royal priesthood, a holy nation, a people belonging to God, that you may declare the praises of him who called you out of darkness into his wonderful light." (1 Peter 2:9)*

REFLECT: _____

_____

_____

_____

_____

_____

_____

_____

_____

_____

_____

_____

DAY 6 Use the following space to write any thoughts God has put in your heart and mind about the things discussed during session six and/or during your Reflections time this week.

SUMMARY: _____

_____

_____

_____

_____

_____

_____

_____

_____

_____

_____

_____

APPENDIX

FREQUENTLY ASKED QUESTIONS

WHAT DO WE DO ON THE FIRST NIGHT OF OUR GROUP?

Like all fun things in life—have a party! A "get to know you" coffee, dinner, or dessert is a great way to launch a new study. You may want to review the Small Group Agreement (pages 89–90) and share the names of a few friends you can invite to join you. But most importantly, have fun before your study time begins.

WHERE DO WE FIND NEW MEMBERS FOR OUR GROUP?

This can be troubling, especially for new groups that have only a few people or for existing groups that lose a few people along the way. We encourage you to pray with your group and then brainstorm a list of people from work, church, your neighborhood, your children's school, family, the gym, and so forth. Then have each group member invite several of the people on his or her list. Another good strategy is to ask church leaders to make an announcement or allow a bulletin insert.

No matter how you find members, it's vital that you stay on the lookout for new people to join your group. All groups tend to go through healthy attrition—the result of moves, releasing new leaders, ministry opportunities, and so forth—and if the group gets too small, it could be at risk of shutting down. If you and your group stay open, you'll be amazed at the people God sends your way. The next person just might become a friend for life. You never know!

HOW LONG WILL THIS GROUP MEET?

It's totally up to the group—once you come to the end of this six-week study. Most groups meet weekly for at least their first six weeks, but every other week can work as well. We strongly recommend that the group meet for the first six months on a weekly basis if at all possible. This allows for continuity, and if people miss a meeting they aren't gone for a whole month.

At the end of this study, each group member may decide if he or she wants to continue on for another six-week study. Some groups launch relationships for years to come, and others are stepping-stones into another group experience. Either way, enjoy the journey.

CAN WE DO THIS STUDY ON OUR OWN?

Absolutely! This may sound crazy but one of the best ways to do this study is not with a full house but with a few friends. You may choose to gather with one other couple who would enjoy going to the movies or having a quiet dinner and then walking through this study. Jesus will be with you even if there are only two of you (Matthew 18:20).

WHAT IF THIS GROUP IS NOT WORKING FOR US?

You're not alone! This could be the result of a personality conflict, life stage difference, geographical distance, level of spiritual maturity, or any number of things. Relax. Pray for God's direction, and at the end of this six-week study, decide whether to continue with this group or find another. You don't buy the first car you look at or marry the first person you date, and the same goes with a group. Don't bail out before the six weeks are up—God might have something to teach you. Also, don't run from conflict or prejudge people before you have given them a chance. God is still working in you too!

WHO IS THE LEADER?

Most groups have an official leader. But ideally, the group will mature and members will rotate the leadership of meetings. We have discovered that healthy groups rotate hosts/leaders and homes on a regular basis. This model ensures that all members grow, give their unique contribution, and develop their gifts. This study guide and the Holy Spirit can keep things on track even when you rotate leaders. Christ has promised to be in your midst as you gather. Ultimately, God is your leader each step of the way.

HOW DO WE HANDLE THE CHILD-CARE NEEDS IN OUR GROUP?

Very carefully. Seriously, this can be a sensitive issue. We suggest that you empower the group to openly brainstorm solutions. You may try one option that works for a while and then adjust over time. Our favorite approach is for adults to meet in the living room or dining room, and to share the cost of a babysitter (or two) who can be with the kids in a different part of the house. In this way, parents don't have to be away from their children all evening when their children are too young to be left at home. A second option is to use one home for the kids and a second home (close by or a phone call away) for the adults. A third idea is to rotate the responsibility of providing a lesson or care for the children either in the same home or in another home nearby. This can be an incredible blessing for kids. Finally, the most common idea is to decide that you need to have a night to invest in your spiritual lives individually or as a couple, and to make your own arrangements for child care. No matter what decision the group makes, the best approach is to dialogue openly about both the problem and the solution.

SMALL GROUP AGREEMENT

OUR PURPOSE

To transform our spiritual lives by cultivating our spiritual health in a healthy small group community. In addition, we: _____

_____

_____

_____

OUR VALUES

Group Attendance	To give priority to the group meeting. We will call or email if we will be late or absent. (Completing the Small Group Calendar on page 91 will minimize this issue.)
Safe Environment	To help create a safe place where people can be heard and feel loved. (Please, no quick answers, snap judgments, or simple fixes.)
Respect Differences	To be gentle and gracious to people with different spiritual maturity, personal opinions, temperaments, or imperfections. We are all works in progress.
Confidentiality	To keep anything that is shared strictly confidential and within the group, and to avoid sharing improper information about those outside the group.
Encouragement for Growth	To be not just takers but givers of life. We want to spiritually multiply our life by serving others with our God-given gifts.

Welcome for Newcomers	To keep an open chair and share Jesus' dream of finding a shepherd for every sheep.
Shared Ownership	To remember that every member is a minister and to ensure that each attender will share a small team role or responsibility over time.
Rotating Hosts/Leaders and Homes	To encourage different people to host the group in their homes, and to rotate the responsibility of facilitating each meeting. (See the Small Group Calendar on page 91.)

OUR EXPECTATIONS

- Refreshments/mealtimes _____
- Child care _____
- When we will meet (day of week) _____
- Where we will meet (place) _____
- We will begin at (time) _____ and end at _____
- We will do our best to have some or all of us attend a worship service together. Our primary worship service time will be _____
- Date of this agreement _____
- Date we will review this agreement again _____
- Who (other than the leader) will review this agreement at the end of this study _____

SMALL GROUP CALENDAR

Planning and calendaring can help ensure the greatest participation at every meeting. At the end of each meeting, review this calendar. Be sure to include a regular rotation of host homes and leaders, and don't forget birthdays, socials, church events, holidays, and mission/ministry projects.

Date	Lesson	Host Home	Dessert/Meal	Leader
Monday, January 15	1	Steve/Laura's	Joe	Bill

PERSONAL HEALTH PLAN

This worksheet could become your single most important feature in this study. On it you can record your personal priorities before the Father. It will help you live a healthy spiritual life, balancing all five of God's purposes.

PURPOSE	PLAN
CONNECT	WHO are you connecting with spiritually?
GROW	WHAT is your next step for growth?
DEVELOP	WHERE are you serving?
SHARE	WHEN are you shepherding another in Christ?
SURRENDER	HOW are you surrendering your heart?

DATE	MY PROGRESS	PARTNER'S PROGRESS

SAMPLE
PERSONAL HEALTH PLAN

This worksheet could become your single most important feature in this study. On it you can record your personal priorities before the Father. It will help you live a healthy spiritual life, balancing all five of God's purposes.

PURPOSE	PLAN
CONNECT	WHO are you connecting with spiritually? *Bill and I will meet weekly by email or phone*
GROW	WHAT is your next step for growth? *Regular devotions or journaling my prayers 2x/week*
DEVELOP	WHERE are you serving? *Serving in Children's Ministry* *Go through GIFTS Class*
SHARE	WHEN are you shepherding another in Christ? *Shepherding Bill at lunch or hosting a starter group in the fall*
SURRENDER	HOW are you surrendering your heart? *Help with our teenager* *New job situation*

DATE	MY PROGRESS	PARTNER'S PROGRESS
3/5	Talked during our group	Figured out our goals together
3/12	Missed our time together	Missed our time together
3/26	Met for coffee and review of my goals	Met for coffee
4/10	Emailed prayer requests	Bill sent me his prayer requests
3/5	Great start on personal journaling	Read Mark 1 – 6 in one sitting!
3/12	Traveled and not doing well this week	Journaled about Christ as Healer
3/26	Back on track	Busy and distracted; asked for prayer
3/1	Need to call Children's Pastor	
3/26	Group did a serving project together	Agreed to lead group worship
3/30	Regularly rotating leadership	Led group worship — great job!
3/5	Called Jim to see if he's open to joining our group	Wanted to invite somebody, but didn't
3/12	Preparing to start a group in fall	
3/30	Group prayed for me	Told friend something he's learning about Christ
3/5	Overwhelmed but encouraged	Scared to lead worship
3/15	Felt heard and more settled	Issue with wife
3/30	Read book on teens	Glad he took on his fear

PERSONAL HEALTH ASSESSMENT

| | JUST BEGINNING | GETTING GOING | WELL DEVELOPED |

CONNECTING WITH GOD AND OTHERS

I am deepening my understanding of and friendship with God in community with others.	1	2	3	4	5
I am growing in my ability both to share and to show my love to others.	1	2	3	4	5
I am willing to share my real needs for prayer and support from others.	1	2	3	4	5
I am resolving conflict constructively and am willing to forgive others.	1	2	3	4	5

CONNECTING TOTAL _____

GROWING IN YOUR SPIRITUAL JOURNEY

I have a growing relationship with God through regular time in the Bible and in prayer (spiritual habits).	1	2	3	4	5
I am experiencing more of the characteristics of Jesus Christ (love, patience, gentleness, courage, self-control, and so forth) in my life.	1	2	3	4	5
I am avoiding addictive behaviors (food, television, busyness, and the like) to meet my needs.	1	2	3	4	5
I am spending time with a Christian friend (spiritual partner) who celebrates and challenges my spiritual growth.	1	2	3	4	5

GROWING TOTAL _____

SERVING WITH YOUR GOD-GIVEN DESIGN

I have discovered and am further developing my unique God-given design.	1	2	3	4	5
I am regularly praying for God to show me opportunities to serve him and others.	1	2	3	4	5
I am serving in a regular (once a month or more) ministry in the church or community.	1	2	3	4	5
I am a team player in my small group by sharing some group role or responsibility.	1	2	3	4	5

SERVING TOTAL _____

SHARING GOD'S LOVE IN EVERYDAY LIFE

I am cultivating relationships with non-Christians and praying
for God to give me natural opportunities to share his love. 1 2 3 4 5

I am praying and learning about where God can use me
and my group cross-culturally for missions. 1 2 3 4 5

I am investing my time in another person or group who
needs to know Christ. 1 2 3 4 5

I am regularly inviting unchurched or unconnected
friends to my church or small group. 1 2 3 4 5

SHARING TOTAL _____

SURRENDERING YOUR LIFE TO GOD

I am experiencing more of the presence and
power of God in my everyday life. 1 2 3 4 5

I am faithfully attending services and my
small group to worship God. 1 2 3 4 5

I am seeking to please God by surrendering every
area of my life (health, decisions, finances,
relationships, future, and the like) to him. 1 2 3 4 5

I am accepting the things I cannot change and
becoming increasingly grateful for the life I've been given. 1 2 3 4 5

SURRENDERING TOTAL _____

	Connecting	Growing	Developing	Sharing	Surrendering	
20						Well Developed
16						Very Good
12						Getting Good
8						Fair
4						Just Beginning

○ Beginning Assessment Total _____   ☐ Ending Assessment Total _____

TELLING YOUR STORY

First, don't underestimate the power of your testimony. Revelation 12:11 (TLB) says, "They defeated [Satan] by the blood of the Lamb and by their testimony; for they did not love their lives but laid them down for Him."

A simple three-point approach is very effective in communicating your personal testimony. The approach focuses on (1) what your life was like before you trusted Christ, (2) how you surrendered to him, and (3) the difference in you since you've been walking with him. If you became a Christian at a very young age and don't remember what life was like before Christ, reflect on what you have seen in the lives of others. Before you begin, pray and ask God to give you the right words.

BEFORE YOU KNEW CHRIST

Simply tell what your life was like before you surrendered to Christ. What was the key problem, emotion, situation, or attitude you were dealing with? What motivated you? What were your actions? How did you try to satisfy your inner needs? Create an interesting picture of your pre-conversion life and problems, and then explain what created a need and interest in Christian things.

HOW YOU CAME TO KNOW CHRIST

How were you converted? Simply tell the events and circumstances that caused you to consider Christ as the solution to your needs. Take time to identify the steps that brought you to the point of trusting Christ. Where were you? What was happening at the time? What people or problems influenced your decision?

THE DIFFERENCE CHRIST HAS MADE IN YOUR LIFE

What is different about your life in Christ? How has his forgiveness impacted you? How have your thoughts, attitudes, and emotions changed?

What problems have been resolved or changed? Share how Christ is meeting your needs and what a relationship with him means to you now. This should be the largest part of your story.

TIPS

- Don't use evangelical jargon: don't sound churchy, preachy, or pious.
- Stick to the point. Your conversion and new life in Christ should be the main points.
- Be specific. Include events, genuine feelings, and personal insights — both before and after conversion — which people would be interested in and that clarify your main point. This makes your testimony easier to relate to. Assume you are sharing with someone with no knowledge of the Christian faith.
- Be current. Tell what is happening in your life with God now, today.
- Be honest. Don't exaggerate or portray yourself as living a perfect life with no problems. This is not realistic. The simple truth of what God has done in your life is all the Holy Spirit needs to convict someone of their sin and convince them of his love and grace.
- Remember, it's the Holy Spirit that convicts. You need only be obedient and tell your story.
- When people reply to your efforts to share with statements like "I don't believe in God," "I don't believe the Bible is God's Word," or "How can a loving God allow suffering?" how can we respond to these replies?
  — Above all, keep a positive attitude. Don't be defensive.
  — Be sincere. This will speak volumes about your confidence in your faith.
  — Don't be offended. It's not you they are rejecting.
  — Pray silently, on-the-spot. Don't proceed without asking for God's help about the specific question. Seek his guidance on how, or if, you should proceed at this time.
  — In God's wisdom, choose to do one of the following:
      (1) Postpone sharing at this time.
      (2) Answer their objections, if you can.
      (3) Promise to research their questions and return answers later.

LEADING FOR THE FIRST TIME

- **Sweaty palms are a healthy sign.** The Bible says God is gracious to the humble. Remember who is in control; the time to worry is when you're not worried. Those who are soft in heart (and sweaty palmed) are those whom God is sure to speak through.

- **Seek support.** Ask your leader, coleader, or close friend to pray for you and prepare with you before the session. Walking through the study will help you anticipate potentially difficult questions and discussion topics.

- **Bring your uniqueness to the study.** Lean into who you are and how God wants you to uniquely lead the study.

- **Prepare. Prepare. Prepare.** Read the Introduction and Leader's Notes for the session you are leading. Consider writing in a journal or fasting for a day to prepare yourself for what God wants to do.

- **Don't wait until the last minute to prepare.**

- **Ask for feedback so you can grow.** Perhaps in an email or on cards handed out at the study, have everyone write down three things you did well and one thing you could improve on. Don't get defensive, but show an openness to learn and grow.

- **Prayerfully consider launching a new group.** This doesn't need to happen overnight, but God's heart is for this to happen over time. Not all Christians are called to be leaders or teachers, but we are all called to be "shepherds" of a few someday.

- **Share with your group what God is doing in your heart.** God is searching for those whose hearts are fully his. Share your trials and victories. We promise that people will relate.

INTRODUCTION

Congratulations! You have responded to the call to help shepherd Jesus' flock. There are few other tasks in the family of God that surpass the contribution you will be making. As you prepare to lead this small group, there are a few thoughts to keep in mind:

Review the "Read Me First" on pages 9–11 so you'll understand the purpose of each section in the study. If this is your first time leading a small group, turn to Leading for the First Time section on page 100 of the appendix for suggestions.

Remember that you are not alone. God knows everything about you, and he knew that you would be leading this group. God promises, "Never will I leave you; never will I forsake you" (Hebrews 13:5b).

Your role as leader. Create a safe warm environment for your group. As a leader, your most important job is to create an atmosphere where people are willing to talk honestly about what the topics discussed in this study have to do with them. Be available before people arrive so you can greet them at the door. People are naturally nervous at a new group, so a hug or handshake can help put them at ease.

Prepare for each meeting ahead of time. Review the Leader's Notes and write down your responses to each study question. Pay special attention to exercises that ask group members to do something other than engage in discussion. These exercises will help your group live what the Bible teaches, not just talk about it. Be sure you understand how an exercise works, and bring any necessary supplies (such a paper or pens) to your meeting.

Pray for your group members by name. Before you begin each session, go around the room in your mind and pray for each member by name. You may want to review the prayer list at least once a week. Ask God to use your time together to touch the heart of every person uniquely. Expect God to lead you to those he wants you to encourage or challenge in a special way.

Discuss expectations. Ask everyone to tell what he or she hopes to get out of this study. You might want to review the Small Group Agreement (see pages 89–90) and talk about each person's expectations and priorities. You could discuss whether you want to do the For Deeper Study for homework before each meeting. Review the Small Group Calendar on page 91 and talk about who else is willing to open their home to host or facilitate a meeting.

Don't try to go it alone. Pray for God to help you, and enlist help from the members of your group. You will find your experience to be richer and more rewarding if you enable group members to help — and you'll be able to help group members discover their individual gifts for serving or even leading the group.

Plan a kick-off meeting. We recommend that you plan a kick-off meeting where you will pray, hand out study guides, spend some time getting to know each other, and discuss each person's expectations for the group. A meeting like this is a great way to start a group or step up people's commitments.

A simple meal, potluck, or even good desserts make a kick-off meeting more fun. After dessert, have everyone respond to an icebreaker question, such as, "How did you hear of our church, and what's one thing you love about it?" Or, "Tell us three things about your life growing up that most people here don't know."

If you aren't able to hold a "get to know you" meeting before you launch into session one, consider starting the first meeting half an hour early to give people time to socialize without shortchanging your time in the study. For example, you can have social time from 7:00 to 7:30, and by 7:40 you'll gather the group with a prayer. Even if only a few people are seated in the living room by 7:40, ask them to join you in praying for those who are coming and for God to be present among you as you meet. Others will notice you praying and will come and sit down. You may want to softly play music from a LIFE TOGETHER Worship CD or other worship CD as people arrive and then turn up the volume when you are ready to begin. This first night will set the tone for the whole six weeks.

You may ask a few people to come early to help set up, pray, and introduce newcomers to others. Even if everyone is new, they don't know that yet and may be shy when they arrive. You might give people roles like setting up name tags or handing out drinks. This could be a great way to spot a coleader.

Subgrouping. If your group has more than seven people, break into discussion groups of two to four people for the Growing and Surrendering sections each week. People will connect more with the study and each other when they have more opportunity to participate. Smaller discussion circles encourage quieter people to talk more and tend to minimize the effects of more vocal or dominant members. Also, people who are unaccustomed to praying aloud will feel more comfortable praying within a smaller group of people. Consider sharing prayer requests in the larger group and then break into smaller groups to pray for each other. People are more willing to pray in small circles if they know that the whole group will hear all the prayer requests.

Memorizing Scripture. Although we have not provided specific verses for the group to memorize, this is something you can encourage the group to do each week. One benefit of memorizing God's Word is noted by the psalmist in Psalm 119:11: "I have hidden your word in my heart that I might not sin against you."

Anyone who has memorized Scripture can confirm the amazing spiritual benefits that result from this practice. Don't miss out on the opportunity to encourage your group to grow in the knowledge of God's Word through Scripture memorization.

Reflections. We've provided opportunity for a personal time with God using the Reflections at the end of each session. Don't press seekers to do this, but just remind the group that every believer should have a plan for personal time with God.

Invite new people. Finally, cast the vision, as Jesus did, to be inclusive not exclusive. Ask everyone to prayerfully think of people who would enjoy or benefit from a group like this. The beginning of a new study is a great time to welcome a few people into your circle. Have each person share a name or two and either make phone calls the coming week or handwrite invitations or postcards that very night. This will make it fun and also make it happen. Don't worry about ending up with too many people—you can always have one discussion circle in the living room and another in the dining room.

SESSION 1: FESTIVE INFLUENCE — LEVI, JESUS, AND THE SINNERS

If your group is new and you aren't able to hold a "get to know you" meeting before you launch into session one, consider starting this first meeting half an hour early to give people time to socialize without shortchanging your time in the study. For example, you can have social time from 7:00 to 7:30, and by 7:40 you'll gather the group with a prayer. Open your group time in prayer each week. Even if only a few people are seated in the living room by 7:40, ask them to join you in praying for those who are coming and for God to be present among you as you meet. Others will notice you praying and will come and sit down. This first night will set the tone for the whole six weeks.

CONNECTING. Question 1. Take some time now to briefly share with the group how you came to be here today. Get the group started by telling how *you* usually respond when invited to parties or other social events with people you don't know. You will get to know each other more quickly if you spend time with an icebreaker question at each session. This is a great opportunity for bonding within your group.

Question 2. With any group, whether you are just forming or have been together for a while, it's good to review and consider your shared values from time to time. On pages 89 – 90 you'll find a Small Group Agreement delineating those values we have found over the years to be the most useful in building and sustaining healthy, balanced groups.

Take some time to review this agreement before your meeting. Then during your meeting, read the agreement aloud to the entire group. If someone has concerns about a specific item or the agreement as a whole, be sensitive to their questions. Explain that tens of thousands of groups use agreements like this one as a simple tool for building trust and group health over time. Some of the items in the agreement, such as "Welcome for Newcomers" and "Shared Ownership," will become clearer during the six sessions of the study. It's a good idea to pick one or two values you haven't focused on before to guide you through this study.

Likewise, take time before your group meets to review the Frequently Asked Questions on pages 86 – 88 and prepare yourself for any questions the group may have about them.

Question 3. Come to the meeting prepared to begin collecting information for your group roster. You might want to make a copy of the Small Group Roster on pages 120–121 of this study guide and then pass it around the group during the discussion. Have everyone write down their contact information and then ask someone to make copies or type up a list with everyone's information and email it to the group this week.

GROWING. Have someone read the introductory stories and Bible passages aloud. It's a good idea to ask someone ahead of time, because not everyone is comfortable reading aloud in public. When the passage has been read, ask the questions that follow. It is not necessary that everyone answer every question in the Bible study. In fact, a group can become boring if you simply go around the circle and give answers. Your goal is to create a discussion—which means that perhaps only a few people respond to each question and an engaging dialogue gets going. It's even fine to skip some questions in order to spend more time on questions you believe are most important.

Question 4. Matthew followed Jesus willingly, turning from his old life to a life of service to Jesus. Even better, he brought his friends to meet Jesus as well. Discuss the ways in which Matthew, in this passage, is an example to all believers.

Question 5. To get group discussion started, you might briefly share one thing you left behind when you became a Christ-follower as an example that, yes, God always asks us to leave *something* behind. It might not be *everything* (our jobs, families, etc.) but it is always our *old selves* (some of our values, priorities, and interests).

Question 6. Matthew probably had great wealth and influence, so he could attract many types of people to his party. Leaving everything behind to follow Jesus makes quite a statement to anyone watching. What a witness! Help your group understand the significance that inviting unbelievers to your parties might make.

Question 7. This question is designed to help group members realize that we need to learn to discern truth from lies. People will attempt to steer us toward their way of thinking and living, but often for their own benefit, not ours. Anyone who doesn't follow God's ways is leading others astray. Motive is everything.

Question 8. Matthew's example is a strong statement for evangelism. We should invite our friends to come and meet Jesus so they can have what we have.

Question 9. The Pharisees were the popular religious party during Jesus' ministry. They were noted for their self-righteousness and their pride. They were bitter and persistent enemies of Jesus. Does this sound like anyone you know? The world cultivates this attitude. It is all around us. Consequently it is not difficult to fall into its trap if we are not careful.

Question 10. Time in God's Word will help us to know who we are and why we need Jesus.

Question 11. Just as a person must recognize he is sick before seeking the help of a doctor for healing, a person must see that he is a sinner in order to be saved. The outward manifestation of repentance will look different in each person's life, as each is afflicted differently.

Question 12. Recognizing our sin helps us see where change is needed in our lives. As we strive for change, we also grow in character. Our sense of right and wrong becomes more in line with God's views than the world's views.

FOR DEEPER STUDY. As leader, we highly recommend that you read the For Deeper Study section and any associated Leader's Notes before the meeting. Plan to draw the group's attention to anything that will help them understand the Bible passages being studied.

In 2 Corinthians 6:14, Paul urges believers not to form binding relationships with unbelievers because this might weaken their Christian commitment, integrity, or standards. He is not saying we should avoid relationships with nonbelievers. In fact, in 1 Corinthians 5:9–11 Paul explained his thinking on this. Paul even tells Christians to stay with their unbelieving spouses in 1 Corinthians 7:12–13. Believers should be active in their witness for Christ to nonbelievers, but they should not build personal or business relationships that could cause them to compromise their faith.

DEVELOPING. Question 13. For many, spiritual partners will be a new idea. We highly encourage you to pair up group members for this study. It's so hard to start a spiritual practice like prayer, consistent Bible reading, or sharing your faith, without support. A friend makes a huge difference. We call this connection a "spiritual partnership." We encourage you to give partners time to check in during the Connecting time of each meeting, however, they can check in with each other weekly between meetings as well. As leader, you may want to prayerfully decide who would be a good match with whom. Let people know that this partnership isn't forever; it's just for a few weeks.

In a week or two, you might want to ask the group how their partnerships are going. This will encourage those who are struggling to connect or accomplish their goals.

In this session we encourage you to become familiar with and encourage group members to use the Personal Health Plan to challenge and track their spiritual goals and progress as well as their partner's. There is one Personal Health Plan in the appendix of this book, but be sure to have a few extra copies on hand at your first meeting for groups of three spiritual partners.

Question 14. Another appendix item to review before your group meeting is Telling Your Story on pages 98–99. During the course of this study we will ask you to have your group turn there and practice sharing the various parts of their stories with their spiritual partners or a small circle of group members. Turn there now and review the instructions for learning to tell about how you met Christ and what that has meant in your life. In this session, encourage group members to think and talk about what their lives were like before they knew Christ. (Encourage those who haven't yet committed to Christ or are not sure to look at the information about this in the Surrendering section.) For those who became a Christian at a very young age and don't remember what life was like before Christ, have them reflect on what they have observed in the life of someone close to them. Encourage group members to begin to write out their stories.

SHARING. Question 15. Share your life-changing encounter with the Lord, and pray for opportunities this week to share your story with at least one other person who needs to meet Jesus.

Question 16. A key exercise in this session is the Circles of Life diagram. Everyone in your group already interacts with at least a few unbelievers in the course of their daily life. You don't have to travel thousands of miles away to share your faith—you are already surrounded by people who need to see Christ in you and hear your story. Look at the Circles of Life, located on page 19 of this study guide, before your meeting and identify at least half a dozen names you would write in those circles. Then, when your group gets to this part, you can share with them the people you listed and encourage them to complete their circles as well.

SURRENDERING. Question 17. Review the information in this question before your meeting so you are familiar with its content. Take this opportunity to remind group members what it means to be a follower of Christ and to invite anyone in your group who hasn't yet committed his or her life to Christ to do so now.

If someone in your group prays this prayer for the first time, as a group, congratulate him or her and let them know that they can come to you or anyone in the group if they have questions or need help in any way.

Question 18. Let the group share their prayer requests and be sure to use the Prayer and Praise Report on page 22 to record the requests. Having the prayer requests written down will prompt you to pray for each member. It will also serve as a reminder to you of God's faithfulness as your group sees the prayers answered. After requests have been recorded, spend some time praying as a group for the requests.

Never pressure a person to pray aloud. That's a sure way to scare someone away from your group. Instead of praying in a circle (which makes it obvious when someone stays silent), allow open time when anyone can pray who wishes to do so.

Question 19. Remind the group about the importance of spending time alone with God throughout the week. Mention that the Reflections section can be an opportunity for developing this important habit during this study.

SESSION 2: UNSTAINED INFLUENCE—DANIEL

Most small groups are not led by just one person. Maybe you've been carrying the whole load and you're thinking, *How come nobody told me this? How come nobody's told my group this? They expect me to do everything!* Maybe you've opened your home, bought the materials, prepared the refreshments, led the study, and done all the cleanup. That's a huge burden on a leader. And ironically, it also keeps everyone else from growing in their gifts. During the Developing section of this session you will have an opportunity to include your group members in all the aspects of making your group successful. Give some thought to the roles of leadership your group might be able to take on and be ready to discuss them in question 13.

CONNECTING. Question 1. Checking in with spiritual partners will be an option in all sessions from now on. You'll need to watch the clock and keep these conversations to ten minutes. If partners want more time together (as is ideal), they can connect before, after, or outside meetings. Give them a two-minute notice and hold to it if you ever want to get them back in the circle! If some group members are absent or newcomers have joined you, you may need to help people connect with partners.

This week, ask partners to talk about how their quiet time went this week. They should set and record a goal under the "WHAT is your next step for growth?" question in the Personal Health Plan on page 92.

Question 2. If you prefer (and especially if there are many newcomers), use this lighter icebreaker question for the whole group. We encourage you, though, to let partners check in at least every other week so that those relationships grow solid. Please don't miss this opportunity to take your people deeper. Remember that the goal here is "transforming lives through community," and one-on-one time has an enormous return on time spent.

GROWING. Question 3. Considering Daniel's limited options, it was quite courageous to refuse to eat. But the first portion of the royal food was offered to idols and that made the food contaminated under Mosaic law. Daniel was faithful to God and God was there for Daniel. Such obedience demonstrated Daniel's love for God.

Question 4. The Bible is our guidebook for living a life that is pleasing to God. The Bible is the source; a sermon is an interpretation.

Questions 5 – 7. Paul was probably quoting the Corinthian congregation. Freedom can get carried away to indulgence. Encourage restraint lest we seek our own good over that of others. Daniel was respectful to the palace official and offered him an option to overcome the issue at hand. We can learn much from this technique when opposing someone else. As a result of Daniel's faithful choices, God gave him what he needed to prosper in a situation not of his choosing.

Question 8. Every day in our Christian walk we turn down more popular choices to follow Christ. It's the nature of the Christian life. God wants us to surrender to him every day; he will give us the strength we need to persevere and promises us a place with him in heaven.

Question 9. We become an example for God. Even the king noted Daniel's "continual service" to God when he ordered him thrown into the den of lions (Daniel 6:16).

Question 10. What's in the news today? Leader, check this in advance of the meeting and be ready with examples to discuss.

Questions 11 – 12. They obeyed the Word of God over that of the king to remain true. It was their only option. We cannot rationalize that outward sin or direct disobedience to God is okay as long as we remain true in our hearts. Life on earth brings this figurative fire with it every day. We all face things that threaten our comfort, well-being, and our faith. We can't face them alone. When we try, we run the risk of breaking under the heat.

FOR DEEPER STUDY. As leader, we highly recommend that you read the For Deeper Study section and any associated Leader's Notes before the meeting. Plan to draw the group's attention to anything that will help them understand the Bible passages being studied.

Daniel and his friends' names were changed to make them Babylonian and help them assimilate into the culture. The king also probably hoped to change the religious loyalty of these young men.

DEVELOPING. Question 13. Familiarize yourself with the Personal Health Assessment on pages 96–97 of the appendix before the meeting. You may want to take the assessment yourself ahead of time and think about the roles your group members can take within the group. Ask your coleader or a trusted friend to review it with you. Then you'll understand the power of this tool and the support you can gain from a using it to evaluate your spiritual health.

During the group meeting, have group members complete the Personal Health Assessment and encourage them to take an active role in serving within the group. Record plans and dates on the Small Group Calendar on page 91 of the appendix.

Question 14. This is a very important part of this study—having a Matthew party. As a group, begin planning a party, like the one Matthew held, to which you invite neighbors and friends who may not yet know Christ. Your goal will be to make him known to them by letting them into your life. This means meeting people, getting to know them, allowing them to get to know you, and being ready to share your stories with them. Set a date, place, and theme for your party during this meeting, and ask someone to volunteer to bring invitations to your group meeting next week or have everyone supply their own if this works out better for your group. Party theme ideas include sports (football, Super Bowl), fiesta, luau, western, music, holiday, getting-to-know-you, game night, block party, barbecue, mystery party, decade party ('50s, '60s, '70s), food party (banana split, cookie exchange, pizza, picnic) or season party (winter, spring, summer, fall). Be creative and have fun with this.

SHARING. Question 15. We recommend that you ask group members to sit in circles of two or three people for this discussion so that everyone will have an opportunity to share. Turn to Telling Your Story on pages 98–99 of the appendix and review the "How You Came to Know Christ" section prior to the group meeting so that you can answer any questions that might come up during group time. Encourage group members to write out this aspect of their testimony as they work through it.

SURRENDERING. Question 16. Have everyone answer the question: How can we pray for you this week? Write prayer requests on the Prayer and Praise Report provided on page 36. Close your time together by praying for the needs expressed today, remembering God's power is available to meet them. Also, commit to start praying daily for the party you are planning. Pray for the hearts of those you invite and for strength to share with them before, during, and after your party.

Question 17. Encourage group members to use the Reflections verses at the end of this session in their quiet time this week and to record any thoughts or direction they receive from the Lord in the space provided.

SESSION 3: UNITED INFLUENCE—PETER AND CORNELIUS

In order to maximize your time together and honor the diversity of personality types, do your best to begin and end your group on time. You may even want to adjust your starting or stopping time. Don't hesitate to open in prayer even before everyone is seated. This isn't disrespectful of those who are still gathering — it respects those who are ready to begin, and the others won't be offended. An opening prayer can be as simple as, "Welcome, Lord! Help us! Now let's start."

CONNECTING. Question 1. Don't skip this question; we will use the results of this discussion later in the session. Not everyone needs to share, but we want to be sure everyone has thought about this.

Question 2. If you have time, have spiritual partners pair up for this question. If time is short, share the question with the group as a whole and have a few people give their answers.

GROWING. Remember that your group may become boring if you let every group member answer a question. Two or three responses are plenty.

Question 3. As we discussed in session one, stories have enormous power for witnessing. By communicating that he knew Jewish law but was following God's instructions, Peter was revealing his motives. How people perceive us when we share is important.

Questions 4–5. Cornelius was a devout believer in God and when God sent a vision instructing him to send for Simon Peter, he responded and then eagerly awaited the forthcoming message. Then, as Cornelius's messengers arrived where Peter was staying, Peter was having a vision of his own (Acts 10:13–16). Acts 10:34 explains what Peter learned from his vision. Encourage discussion about times when group members have clearly seen God's hand arranging circumstances in their lives.

Question 6. God saw someone who loved him and needed to know Jesus. God knew that Cornelius's faith would influence many others to be saved as well.

Questions 7–8. God doesn't show favoritism — it's all about what's in your heart. He wants us to know that we are all his people and are all in need of a Savior. He meets us where we are and he wants us to do the same for others, making them more open to him.

Question 9. God's will prevails regardless of what we do. However, we don't get to be a part of what God is doing when we're disobedient. Peter got to experience the joy of seeing Cornelius's household and friends come to know Christ. What could be better than that?

FOR DEEPER STUDY. Draw the group's attention to anything that will help them understand the Bible passages being studied.

The Holy Spirit came upon the house of Cornelius and they believed.

The Lord spoke to David, telling him not to let appearances (Goliath's size, Jewish law) deter him from the task God had placed before him. We need to listen to what God says to us with an open attitude.

DEVELOPING. Question 11. Encourage the group to recognize the circle of influence around their lives; these are the people they should invite to your party. Encourage group members to consider Christian friends as well. They can allow a greater Christian influence at the festivities while group members are busy in their various roles (to be discussed in a future session).

SHARING. Question 12. This question is to get group members thinking about the person who opens their heart and home to people needing Jesus. We often need to be reminded that this is the right thing to do. It's too easy for us to get comfortable with our Christian friends and activities and neglect to include the unchurched or unbelieving people around us in our lives. How can we influence them for God if we don't spend any time with them?

Question 13. As leader, you should review the "Tips" section of Telling Your Story yourself in advance and be ready to share your ideas with the group.

SURRENDERING. Question 14. Share your prayer requests within the group. Then close your time together by praying for one another to overcome any hang-ups that might be keeping you from making an important attitude adjustment in your life. Write down group members' prayer requests, and any praises that are reported, on the Prayer and Praise Report provided on page 49. Be sure to celebrate how God is working among and through your group.

Question 15. Take time to encourage group members to remain faithful to having a quiet time each day. The Reflections verses at the end of this session provide an opportunity for group members to reflect on what they are learning in your group time. Don't miss this opportunity to encourage your group in this important habit.

SESSION 4: REBORN INFLUENCE — NICODEMUS

If you've had trouble getting through all of the Bible study questions in each session, consider breaking into smaller circles of four or five people for the Bible study (Growing) portion of your meeting. Everyone will get more "airtime," and the people who tend to dominate the discussion will be balanced out. A circle of four doesn't need an experienced leader, and it's a great way to identify and train a coleader.

CONNECTING. Question 1. As leader, you should be the first to answer the questions while others are thinking about how to respond. Be sure to give everyone a chance to answer the questions, because it's a chance for the group to get to know each other. It's not necessary to go around the circle in order. Just ask for volunteers to respond.

Question 2. As you encourage your group members to check in with their spiritual partners this week, you might want to ask the group to share how their partnerships are going. This will encourage those who are struggling to connect or accomplish their goals.

GROWING. Questions 3 – 4. Nicodemus was compelled to seek the truth and knew that Jesus had it; he had to go and personally talk with Jesus to learn more. We need to seek the truth at all cost as well. This is very hard for us, as it must have been for Nicodemus. But our very lives depend on it!

Question 5. Nicodemus must truly have had a heart for God, so he recognized the truth when he heard it. He was drawn to it. Frequently, our personal need to be in control of our situation and destiny causes us to be blinded to truth. Because Jesus was not the kind of Messiah most people expected, the Sanhedrin and other "brethren" didn't recognize him.

Question 7. We cannot control the work of the Spirit but we can, and should, join in it. God is in control; we're not. But he has offered us all the opportunity to be a part of what he is doing in the world.

Question 8. The Jews were blinded by the law and all the regulations that had been formed to keep it. They were so focused on the letter of the law, they failed to see the intent of it.

Question 9. In response to confession of sin, God gave people a way to return to him by looking to a snake lifted up on a pole (Numbers 21:8–9). Jesus was similarly lifted up, on the cross, for all to look to for salvation.

Questions 10–11. We are condemned by unbelief. Often, when asked if they have given their lives to Christ, people will say they have not decided. But they have! When we live in the light of God's truth, others will be drawn in as well.

DEVELOPING. Question 13. It's time to start thinking about what your group will do when you're finished with this study. Now is the time to talk about what study you will do next and ask how many people will be joining you so you can have the books available when you meet for session six.

SHARING. Question 15. This is the most important exercise in learning to share your personal testimony with others. Appoint a timekeeper for each subgroup and give everyone two or three minutes to share. Be watchful of the time. This is such a large part of who we are as Christians that people will have a lot to say if you let them.

SURRENDERING. Bring the group back together for the Surrendering time.

Don't forget to give encouragement when people offer answers. Even if someone's answer is difficult to understand, remember that it takes a tremendous step of faith, especially in new groups, to say something early on. Say something like, "Great!" "Thanks!" "That's super!" Then say, "How about somebody else?" "Does anybody else want to share?" Especially if someone starts to dominate the discussion, say, "How about someone who hasn't shared yet?" Keep things bouncing back and forth.

CONNECTING. Question 2. Take time for your group to sit with their spiritual partners. Encourage them to share their responses to this question. You'll need to watch the clock and keep these conversations to five to six minutes. Give them a two-minute notice and hold to it if you ever want to get them back in the circle! If some group members are absent, you may need to help people connect with other partners for today.

GROWING. Questions 3 – 6. Through John the Baptist's proclamation of who Jesus was (as Jesus passed by), Andrew and the other disciple discovered Jesus' identity and followed him. They believed he was the one John the Baptist spoke of — the Christ. Jesus knew they were seeking the Messiah and wanted to spend time with him to get to know him.

Questions 7 – 8. Select among these questions to the degree you have time.

Questions 9 – 10. It's not always easy to share the gospel with family members. Jesus himself said in Matthew 13:57, "Only in his hometown and in his own house is a prophet without honor." But Andrew went to bring his brother to meet Jesus. Rather than "telling," he "introduced."

FOR DEEPER STUDY. As leader, we highly recommend that you read the For Deeper Study section and any associated Leader's Notes before the meeting. Plan to draw the group's attention to anything that will help them understand the Bible passages being studied.

DEVELOPING. Question 13. How is your party planning going? Take time at this session to finalize the planning. Encourage everyone to take on a role that he or she is comfortable with.

SHARING. Question 14. A key exercise in this study has been sharing your personal testimonies with each other. Everyone in your group should have had some opportunity to share either one-on-one with a spiritual partner or in small circles of two to three people. It's also important to be able to share your confidences and fears about telling your story. Set aside enough time during this session to allow people to do this. Then have a few share their entire testimony with the group. This will help prepare them to boldly share when called upon to do so.

SURRENDERING. Question 15. Spend some time praying and be sure to use the Prayer and Praise Report on page 71 to record the requests. Remember, never pressure a person to pray aloud. Do encourage them to participate with short prayers.

Question 16. Remind the group about the importance of spending time alone with God throughout the week. Mention that the Reflections section can be an opportunity for developing this important habit while using this study.

SESSION 6: ALIEN INFLUENCE — PAUL AND THE GENTILES AT ATHENS

You made it! This is the last session of this study! It's a time to celebrate where you've been and look forward to what's next for each of you. Whether your group is ending or continuing, it's important to celebrate where you have come together. Thank everyone for what they've contributed to the group. You might even give some thought ahead of time to something unique each person has contributed. You can say those things at the beginning of your meeting.

Your goal for this meeting is to finish strong. It's also a time to think about God's final, ultimate purpose for you: surrendering your whole lives to him.

CONNECTING. Question 2. Be sure to have spiritual partners check in with each other this last week of the study.

GROWING. Questions 3 – 6. Paul started out by meeting his listeners where they were. This showed that he took an interest in them and their lives. Paul was prepared! He knew who God is, that he is in control, and how he can be known. Paul recognized the Greeks' UNKNOWN GOD as an opportunity to share with them about the one true God. Paul tells the Greeks that God does not live in temples built by hands, which is exactly what idols are.

Questions 7 – 10. It's important to note here that not everyone wants to hear or accept the message of God's salvation. Even Paul's "eloquent" speech did not cause everyone to accept Christ. Read Matthew 13:18 – 23 for Jesus' explanation of the parable of the sower, told in Matthew 13:3 – 9. (The parable and its interpretation are also found in Luke 8:4 – 8, 11 – 15.) Our job is telling. It is the Holy Spirit who changes lives. So, even though we may not see results, by our standards, every time we share our faith, we can know that God wants everyone to come to repentance (1 Timothy 2:1 – 4; 2 Peter 3:9).

FOR DEEPER STUDY. As leader, we highly recommend that you read the For Deeper Study section and any associated Leader's Notes before the meeting. Plan to draw the group's attention to anything that will help them understand the Bible passages being studied.

Paul emphasized the role of prayer — we are to devote ourselves to prayer for ourselves and others (verse 3), and prayers for boldness in proclaiming the Word of God. Also, we have been given the understanding of the mystery of

Christ and we must conduct ourselves accordingly. The mystery, or secret, refers to the mystery of the church as the body of Christ, composed of saved Jews and Gentiles.

DEVELOPING. Question 11. Continue to take turns sharing your testimonies during this last session. Set a time limit—say two to three minutes.

Question 12. If your group is staying together, hopefully you've chosen your next study. If so, have the study guides available at this last meeting, if possible. It's a good idea to have the group take another look at your Small Group Agreement to see if you want to change anything for the next season of your group. Are all the values working for you, or is there some way your group could be improved by changing your expectations or even living up to one of these values better than you have been? You can make people feel safe talking about things they want to improve by first asking them what they've liked about the group. Set a positive tone. Then make sure people get to disagree respectfully, that everyone understands that they're speaking in confidence and won't be talked about outside the group, and that the goal of any changes will be the spiritual health of everyone. One thing people might want to change is the role they took on in the group. Maybe for the next study, the person who's been handling the prayer list would like to swap with the person who's been heading up the worship. Or maybe you want to add a worship component that you haven't had before. Let people know that the group belongs to them and they all have a say.

SURRENDERING. Question 13. Share with your group one thing you would like God to do in your life as a result of these lessons you have studied together. Record your prayer requests on the Prayer and Praise Report on page 81.

Question 14. Hopefully, the Reflections verses at the end of the sessions in this study have instilled a quiet time habit in your group members. Encourage them to continue in this habit.

SMALL GROUP ROSTER

Name	Address	Phone	Email Address	Team or Role	Church Ministry
Bill Jones	7 Alvalar Street L.F. 92665	766-2255	bjones@aol.com	Socials	children's ministry

(Pass your book around your group at your first meeting to get everyone's name and contact information.)

Name	Address	Phone	Email Address	Team or Role	Church Ministry

Experiencing Christ Together:

Living with Purpose in Community

Brett & Dee Eastman; Todd & Denise Wendorff; Karen Lee-Thorp

Experiencing Christ Together: Living with Purpose in Community is a series of six, six-week study guides that offers small groups a chance to explore Jesus' teaching on the five biblical purposes of the church. By closely examining Christ's life and teaching in the Gospels, the series helps group members walk in the steps of Christ's early followers. Jesus lived every moment following God's purposes for his life, and Experiencing Christ Together helps groups learn how they can do this too. The first book lays the foundation: who Christ is and what he has done for us. Each of the other five books in the series looks at how Jesus trained his followers to live one of the five biblical purposes (fellowship, discipleship, service, evangelism, and worship).

	Softcovers	DVD
Beginning in Christ Together	ISBN: 0-310-24986-4	ISBN: 0-310-26187-2
Connecting in Christ Together	ISBN: 0-310-24981-3	ISBN: 0-310-26189-9
Growing in Christ Together	ISBN: 0-310-24985-6	ISBN: 0-310-26192-9
Serving Like Christ Together	ISBN: 0-310-24984-8	ISBN: 0-310-26194-5
Sharing Christ Together	ISBN: 0-310-24983-X	ISBN: 0-310-26196-1
Surrendering to Christ Together	ISBN: 0-310-24982-1	ISBN: 0-310-26198-8

Pick up a copy today at your favorite bookstore!

Doing Life Together series

Brett & Dee Eastman; Todd & Denise Wendorff;
Karen Lee-Thorp

Based on the five biblical purposes that form the bedrock of Saddleback Church, Doing Life Together will help your group discover what God created you for and how you can turn this dream into an everyday reality. Experience the transformation firsthand as you begin Connecting, Growing, Developing, Sharing, and Surrendering your life together for him.

"Doing Life Together is a groundbreaking study . . . [It's] the first small group curriculum built completely on the purpose-driven paradigm . . . The greatest reason I'm excited about [it] is that I've seen the dramatic changes it produces in the lives of those who study it."

—From the foreword by Rick Warren

Small Group Ministry Consultation

Building a healthy, vibrant, and growing small group ministry is challenging. That's why Brett Eastman and a team of certified coaches are offering small group ministry consultation. Join pastors and church leaders from around the country to discover new ways to launch and lead a healthy Purpose-Driven small group ministry in your church. To find out more information please call 1-800-467-1977.

	Softcover	
Beginning Life Together	ISBN: 0-310-24672-5	ISBN: 0-310-25004-8
Connecting with God's Family	ISBN: 0-310-24673-3	ISBN: 0-310-25005-6
Growing to Be Like Christ	ISBN: 0-310-24674-1	ISBN: 0-310-25006-4
Developing Your SHAPE to Serve Others	ISBN: 0-310-24675-X	ISBN: 0-310-25007-2
Sharing Your Life Mission Every Day	ISBN: 0-310-24676-8	ISBN: 0-310-25008-0
Surrendering Your Life for God's Pleasure	ISBN: 0-310-24677-6	ISBN: 0-310-25009-9
Curriculum Kit	ISBN: 0-310-25002-1	

Life Together Student Edition

Brett Eastman & Doug Fields

The Life Together series is the beginning of a relational journey, from being a member of a group to being a vital part of an unbelievable spiritual community. These books will help you think, talk, dig deep, care, heal, share . . . and have the time of your life! Life . . . together!

The Life Together Student Edition DVD Curriculum combines DVD teaching from well-known youth Bible teachers, as well as leadership training, with the Life Together Student Edition Small Group Series to give a new way to do small group study and ministry with basic training on how to live healthy and balanced lives-purpose driven lives.

Pick up a copy today at your favorite bookstore!

We want to hear from you. Please send your comments about this
book to us in care of zreview@zondervan.com. Thank you.

ZONDERVAN.com/
AUTHORTRACKER
follow your favorite authors